DELUSIONS
OF EVERYDAY
LIFE

DELUSIONS

OF EVERYDAY

LIFE

....

LEONARD SHENGOLD, M.D.

Yale University Press   New Haven and London

Published with assistance from the Mary Cady Tew
Memorial Fund.

Parts of four chapters of this book have previously
been published in different form in *The
Psychoanalytic Quarterly* and *The International
Journal and Review of Psycho-Analysis*

Designed by Sonia L. Scanlon.
Set in Minion type by Keystone Typesetting, Inc.,
Orwigsburg, Pennsylvania.
Printed in the United States of America by Book-
Crafters, Inc., Chelsea, Michigan.

Library of Congress Cataloging-in-Publication Data
Shengold, Leonard.
Delusions of everyday life / Leonard Shengold.
p.   cm.
Includes bibliographical references and index.
ISBN 0-300-06268 (alk. paper)
1. Delusions.   2. Narcissism.   I. Title.
RC553.D35S54   1995
616.89—dc20   94-38368
CIP

A catalogue record for this book is available from the
British Library.

The paper in this book meets the guidelines for
permanence and durability of the Committee on
Production Guidelines for Book Longevity of the
Council on Library Resources.

10 9 8 7 6 5 4 3 2 1

To Maya Sophia Shengold

The nature of amour-propre and of this human self is to love only oneself, to consider only oneself. But what can a man do? He can't keep this object he loves from being full of defects and meanness. He wants to be great, he sees himself small; he wants to be happy, he sees himself wretched; he wants to be perfect, he sees himself full of imperfections; he wants to be the object of men's love and esteem, and he sees that his faults deserve only their aversion and their scorn. This quandary in which he finds himself produces in him the most unjust and criminal passion imaginable, for he conceives a mortal hatred for this truth that reproves him and convinces him of his faults. He would like to annihilate it; and being unable to destroy it in itself *he destroys it, as far as he can, in his own consciousness and in that of others*; that is, he devotes all his care to hiding his defects from others and from himself, and he cannot bear that anyone should see them or show them to him. To be full of faults is no doubt a great evil; but it is a much greater evil to be full of them and unwilling to recognize them, since that is *the extra addition of a voluntary illusion.* [italics added]

Pascal, *Pensées*

CONTENTS

. . . .

ACKNOWLEDGMENTS

· · · · · · ·

In earlier books I have thanked and acknowledged my debt to friends, colleagues, teachers, and, especially, patients. Five very dear friends, my colleagues Shelley Orgel, Austin Silber, Vann Spruiell, Ed Weinshel, and Gladys Topkis (also my editor), have read a preliminary draft of this book and have provided criticism and invaluable suggestions, as has my wife, who has gone over every word of every draft of every chapter. I cannot thank them enough. I am especially beholden to Lawrence Kenney, my fine manuscript editor, for his tactful and invaluable suggestions. I am grateful to Jon Snow and Laurence Shengold for their much needed help with computer problems. I am indebted to David Raby, whose fine biography of Samuel Butler I have learned much from and made much use of in my chapter on Butler.

Looking back on what I have written in the five books that have enlivened my existence over the past seven years, I feel their deficiencies acutely—but also a definite pride in achievement. I have not tried to deliver more than I am capable of. I have presented my own, very personal synthesis of psychoanalytic theory and, especially, practice—the latter based on the relatively few analytic cases that any analyst, and I have been a busy one, can study, even over a working span of nearly forty years. As an encompassing view of human psychology, I have fashioned a covering garment full of holes—blind spots (some of my own delusions of everyday life are operative here), ignorances, and inadequacies. There are many very valuable contributors to psychoanalytic thinking whose work

I know too little or have used inadequately or not at all, and I owe them apologies. In all of my books I have used great literature as well as my clinical practice to illustrate my ideas. Here I have followed Freud's example. Psychoanalytic writers should attend to the great psychologists of the past in their own attempts at exploration. This applies also to what I assume the reader will already be familiar with about delusions of everyday life: in stressing their pathological (destructive and resistant) effects, I have said little about their positive (defensive and adaptive) use. We really could not live without a great measure of delusion and denial. Great literature is full of this message. Ibsen talks of the need for "life illusions" or "vital lies" (*The Wild Duck*); Eugene O'Neill, a lesser playwright, uses a more awkward expression, "pipedreams" (*The Iceman Cometh*). In *The Brothers Karamazov*, Dostoyevsky's Grand Inquisitor speaks of man's need for delusion determining the Church's duty to supply him with "magic, mystery, and authority." And, most elequent of all is Blaise Pascal, who repeatedly reminds us we require illusions and diversion from man's fate and role in a universe of infinities. Freud presents the unconscious as timeless and changeless; and even the wisest masters of reality will sometimes regress to this basic element of psychic reality. The vagaries and the tragedy of the human condition require reassuring transient illusions and delusions of immortality and a fixed universe.

DELUSIONS
OF EVERYDAY
LIFE

INTRODUCTION

. . . .

> But we are parents after all, burdened with all the
> delusions that accompany this condition.
> —Freud, in a letter to his prospective son-in-law,
> Max Halberstadt, July 7, 1912

Reader, look around you and look into yourself. I am trying to emphasize what we, we ordinary people, all know, what we all take for granted—the minor eccentricities and "crazinesses" of our acquaintances and of ourselves.

When I was a psychiatric resident at Kings County Hospital in Brooklyn in the 1950s, I attended lectures on the major psychoses given by an émigré physician and psychoanalyst, Jan Frank. I believe Jan was born in Hungary, but he had lived for many years in Prague and had been trained and practiced psychiatry and psychoanalysis there. He was driven out of his beloved Czechoslovakia by the Nazis and had worked at the Menninger Foundation in Kansas before coming to New York. He was a wonderful teacher and an exhibitionistic but astute interviewer of patients. Usually he could get even the silent ones to respond to his empathic blandishments, and picking out a patient to present to (and who might baffle or stump) Dr. Frank at his weekly ward conference was one of the pleasures of being a chief resident. After what was usually an astounding interview, Jan would subsequently evoke, describe, and invest with meaning for us the clinical phenomena we had witnessed together but that we residents had not always observed properly or understood. His accomplishments, achieved partly by his great gift for mimicry, seemed almost magical. It was a mimicry of bizarre transcription—with the psychotic patients of various ethnic backgrounds who came from Brooklyn and Queens, each speaking in some version of Jan's own thick, wild, and peculiar middle-European accent. Jan Frank was obviously an eccentric. It was hard to picture him as having worked for years at Menninger; he seemed to belong more in Oz than in Kansas. He was different from the rest of us—in his posture and ways of moving, his dress, and his speech. His vaguely Hungarian, very individual way of speaking, full of subtly changing and intermittently explosive vagaries of tone and key, wound itself about a myriad of idiosyncratic (and often, I felt, willful) mispronunciations. His speech flowed largely by way of what I took to be free associations, studded with puns and quotations (the former frequently not based on the English language, the latter usually from classical and hardly ever from familiar or popular literature). The puns often misfired with most or all of the audience, but they always amused Jan, whose appreciative and self-congratulatory chuckling could reach prolonged crescendos of highly pitched cackling. In spite of this, by the time he had finished a teaching session, one could sense that there had indeed been method in his madness—he made us feel what the individual schizophrenic or manic-depressive was like, and above all that these *were* individuals, not just aggregations of symptoms and Bleulerian generalizations. And he taught us that much of their speech and actions could be understood and connected with their human concerns and problems. Their language, which often at first had appeared to us to be gibberish, was revealed in Jan's translations or by his dialogue with the patient (he had a skill here I have never seen equalled) to be for the most part comprehensible communication that marked the essential humanity of the strange creatures whom at first we had treated with defensive and reductive isolation.[1] We learned from Jan that these crazies were not so different from us. This, an essential lesson for anyone who is to try to help the psychotic person, brought with it its own anxieties, but learning to bear and even to learn from them about ourselves as well as our patients was part of our job. I am immensely grateful to Jan for what he helped me to see.

Jan had a unique, unforgettable way of moving—both tic-like and athetoid; his body was in almost constant expressive use. "We Europeans talk with our hands," he announced, somewhat apologetically. But he talked with his hands and his feet and his torso. I wondered if he did not have some mild form of Tourette's syndrome. Face to face with a schizophrenic patient, he would adopt and adapt the patient's speech patterns, expressive gesticulations or immobilities, and form of (primary process) thinking to become a more animated, sometimes caricatured, Hungarian version of a mirror image of the person he was interviewing. When we as new residents, unfamiliar with and still afraid of psychotics, saw this kind of demonstration for the first time, Dr. Frank, in his dramatic and exaggerated kinetic exhibitionism, seemed to us much crazier than the patient. After the interview, he proclaimed with gusto, "I know, you all think I am *meshugga*, right?" (He was right.) "But it is the patient who is *meshugga*. Me, I am just *meshugoid*." It is my thesis in this book that we, even the sanest among us, are all to some extent "meshugoid"—but the two categories can of course coexist in the same person.

This book is not about diagnosis, which I find of limited use (see Shengold 1989); I am not dealing here with the major psychoses. To realize the ubiquity of the delusions of everyday life does not

---

1. "Macbeth's a paranoid psychotic," said one of the colleagues with whom I had just started residency after we had attended a theatrical performance together. I felt he understood neither *Macbeth* nor paranoid psychosis.

require the third ear or the extra eye (*Un Oeil en trop*)[2] of the psychoanalyst. Perception and apperception of this existential "fact" are available to the intelligent observer and self-observer and are documented in the works of great, psychologically adept writers of fiction, biography, and autobiography. Think of the characters and in some cases the life of Shakespeare, Chekhov, Tolstoy, Turgenev, Balzac, Stendhal, Flaubert, Proust, Jane Austen, Dickens, the Brontës, George Eliot, Henry James, Ibsen; of the nonfictional works of Montaigne, Rousseau, Saint-Simon, Herzen; and of the books about the lives of many other great and not so great men and women in all fields. But this book is written not so much to point out what anyone can know, fairly easily about others, reluctantly about oneself. I am stressing the difficulties that the meshugoid traces of the different, vibrantly changing mental functioning of the infant and young child make in the relationships between human beings. I want specifically to focus on the residual infantile emotional currents as these present themselves in the relationship between the psychological therapist and his or her grown-up patient. These currents both motivate and hinder any kind of psychoanalytic work because they profoundly affect the phenomena of transference and resistance, on which clinical psychoanalyses are based.[3] The resistances in treatment sometimes come primarily by way of denial of infantile aspects of the patient's mental representations of self and of parents, as well of others who have (by way of transference) transiently or significantly taken the parents' place. A

2. Title of a book by the psychoanalyst André Green; it is a French translation of a line from a poem by Hölderlin referring to Oedipus.

3. *Transference* refers to the human tendency to "transfer" feelings originally experienced in relation to our earliest meaningful "objects" of instinctual drives and mental interests, the parents, onto others—and therefore onto the therapist or analyst; *resistance* refers to the operation of defensive forces as they come into play in relation to the therapist or analyst in psychological therapy.

patient will often explain away a bizarre character trait, defense, or symptom of his or her own by saying, "Oh, my mother [father] is like that!" This usually turns out to mean (although it is not always stated), "Therefore it doesn't count!" So it is not "owned" (see chapter 7).

I once saw in consultation a woman in her early thirties from the Midwest. Her analyst, whom I did not know, had read my book *Soul Murder*, about child abuse and incest. He had urged her to come to New York and talk to me about her relationship with her father, which apparently had not been very much modified even after years of therapy and analysis. The patient's mother had died just after she reached puberty. She was an only child. Her father had not remarried. The girl had been expected to take over her mother's duties, and in large part she had complied, making a home and acting as hostess for her father. Until recently she had had few friends of her own. It was obvious that she was intelligent, and she had done well scholastically in college but had been socially isolated there. She seemed more a child than a mature woman. Although the father had not, according to her account, actually gone to bed with his daughter, he was always not only joking about it but embracing and trying to fondle her. He wanted her to sleep in his bed, and when they traveled together he had always insisted that she share a double bed in hotels. During the interview she described in detail her father's seductiveness; the words contained complaint and even outrage, but her tone was one of indifference. I had the definite impression of a smile of self-satisfaction as she described her father's attempts and the mixture of compliance and refusal with which she had reacted. Her father had broken up any close relationship she had, not only with boys and men but even with girlfriends. He had retired from his business, and the main purpose of his life appeared to have become the supplying of companionship to his daughter. They became a couple and went everywhere together.

Finally, after several years of treatment, her psychiatrist/analyst had insisted that she move out of the family home, get her own apartment and a job. This she had done, but her job was a menial one, and her earnings were enough just to sustain her living expenses. She had started to find a few girlfriends. Her father, called upon to pay for her treatment, did so reluctantly and was always late in paying, making the analyst wait. As for living apart from him, she complained that her father was always turning up—even waiting for her in her analyst's waiting room. He would plan "nice" mutual vacations that she found hard to resist.

I began to feel some of the frustration her analyst may have felt about the motivation of this pathetic victim of her father's possessive and sexual wishes. She seemed to me to be in a secret, predominantly masochistic, willing, perhaps even enthusiastic, bondage—a bondage that was also a bond, one that enacted some of the revenge and satisfaction involved in frustrating both her father and her analyst. She had somehow managed to reconstitute her early parental situation by getting her analyst and her father to quarrel over her; they, not she, had become responsible for her actions and feelings. I should therefore not have been surprised (and yet it came as a shock) when I noticed that when the patient was talking about her father, she was tossing her head toward my waiting room. I found myself asking, "You don't mean you have come here with your father?" "Oh yes—he's in the waiting room. He insisted on coming. And although he promised to get two hotel rooms he only got one!" This was proclaimed with a triumphant smile. Both the patient and her father were given to similar tendencies, involving all sorts of bizarre manners and practices; they were both full of duplicity for which they took no responsibility and were both subject to what Pascal calls "voluntary illusions."[4] I felt very little

4. See this book's epigraph. The "illusions" are of course not always voluntary; they can be unconscious or something in between.

hope that this woman would ever really be motivated to separate from her father. They were united in their mutual "craziness." I concluded that not only was the patient's separation from her father an as-if operation but so was this consultation, and I feared that her analysis might be yet another.

The patient's wish for change seemed to be accompanied by its opposite. What was "delusional" here was the defensive split whereby there was no way to integrate the contradictory wishes—a vertical split in the mind that is a primitive kind of mental functioning that flourishes in the early time of mental development. The result, in the adult, represents something close to Orwell's "doublethink."[5]

Splitting is one of the primal defensive mechanisms that bring on delusion and delusion-like manifestations; these mechanisms can make conflicts within our minds impossible to *own*—(I repeat what I will be repeating again and again in this book). One cannot analyze what is not there. Freud says, "You must catch your thief before you can hang him" (1909, 124).

I will outline the rest of this book. I assume a basic and simplified version of the Freudian theory of psychic development (emphasized in recent literature in a fine book by Jonathan Lear, *Love and Its Place in Nature*). The mind's primitive functioning, beginning in the very early narcissistic period of mental development, features primary process thinking, intense contradictory (BLACK or WHITE) "primal" affects full of somatic intensity, primal de-

---

5. From *Nineteen Eighty-Four*: "To know and not to know, to be conscious of complete truthfulness while telling carefully constructed lies, to hold simultaneously two opinions which cancelled out, knowing them to be contradictory and believing both . . . to forget whatever it is necessary to forget, then to draw it back into the memory again at the moment it was needed, and then promptly to forget it again, and above all to apply the same process to the process itself . . . consciously to induce unconsciousness, and then once again to become unconscious of the act of hypnosis you had just performed" (1949, 36).

fenses,[6] inadequate separation from a primal parent, possessing only islands of integrative ego. All these, in the course of the development of object relations (psychoanalytic jargon for the inner mental registration of, and achievement of separation from, the parent figures) and mental maturation, become partially transformed into predominantly mature psychic functioning.[7]

Primal functioning never disappears. Some of it can continue with little modification (we call this fixation). What is transformed can, in transient or more lasting regression, return to the old functioning. All of us are left with individually varying fragments of the originally hallucinatory and delusional ways of operating. Hallucinations tend to disappear for most people (except in dreams and some states of altered consciousness, normal and pathological, and in toxic and psychotic conditions), but delusions or near delusions (I call these quasi-delusions) continue for the neurotic majority. These everyday delusions (again, different in degree and intensity and variety for every individual) are seldom clamorous, but they powerfully influence and even motivate thought, feeling, and action.

I am not at all comfortable with my use of the words *delusion* (because of its specific pathological connotations) or even *quasi-delusion*. This dissatisfaction has been mirrored in complaints of several friends with whom I have discussed the problem (or who have read parts of the manuscript of this book). But, unfortunately,

6. These include introjection, projection, identification with the aggressor, idealization, devaluation, denial.

7. Another partial list: primary process thinking is supplemented by secondary process thinking, affects become modulated and more flexible and less associated with massive somatic involvement, a range of defenses evolve; danger situations of less than traumatic intensities, a separated self, and integrative ego functioning emerge. These do not entirely replace the primal functioning but modify and overlay it.

I have not been able to settle on a better term for the psychotic-like remnants of primitive mental processes which continue into adult life. Given that all we know and have mentally is compromise formation (Brenner), these processes are much more complicated than, and include, primal symptoms (such as delusion), primal defenses (such as denial), primal impulses (cannibalistic, murderous, polymorphous perverse, and so on). I have tried to modify my use of *delusion* by sometimes putting it in quotation marks and by using *quasi-delusion* and other more descriptive expressions— the variety does properly denote a range of delusional intensity. But the reader has my apologies for making use of *delusion* not so much in a literal as in a metaphoric sense—and for rhetorical purpose. (I will be attempting to define and discuss these terms at greater length in chapter 2.) Perhaps a better term might be *fixed convictions,* but that seems too nonpathological and lacks the motive power connoted by *delusions.*

I try to deal with "everyday" narcissistic delusions (delusions involving self and parent—of omnipotence, of immortality, of perfection, of being the favorite of the gods [parents]); paranoid delusions; delusions associated with perversions; delusions derived from identification with delusional (psychotic and nonpsychotic) parents—all of which can of course overlap. The chapter on envy centers around why these delusions are needed defensively—to reduce the central preoedipal (which can go on to become the oedipal) burden provided by the intensity of instinctual drives, especially by aggressive destructiveness. I illustrate my ideas with both clinical and literary material (dwelling most on the nineteenth-century English writer Samuel Butler, who has already been the subject of psychoanalytic study by Phyllis Greenacre).

The book has a clinical purpose. I feel that these manifestations of delusional intensity (remnants of primal psychic life) tie us to our early mental impressions of parents, to whom we cling as indispensable to our existence. These "delusions," therefore, also link us to the glorious promise and terrible dangers and affects of that early period—promise and dangers that adhere to the primal parental pillars of our identities. These bonds to a long-ago past give power and form to our resistance to change and maturation in life. (It follows that this is also true for resistances to psychotherapeutic and psychoanalytic treatment; recognizing the delusional intensities can be helpful if not sometimes even necessary for therapist and patient alike.) Finally, the delusions of everyday life can never be eliminated, but they need to be acknowledged and owned[8] before they can be attenuated. This can of course happen in life with maturation, and if maturation is inhibited, some (and sometimes considerable) liberation is possible in psychotherapy. I end the book with a discussion of owning—owning both what we are and what has happened to us—a requisite acquisition in life and therapy toward accepting change and establishing identity and authenticity.

I have given several lectures based on some of the chapters of this book. At two different places, I heard similar responses to the same paper (on malignant envy)—delivered in antithetical critical tones. The first, a denigrating remark for a peer (I attributed the hostility, perhaps unfairly, to *his* malignant envy), was, "Shengold, you have told us things that we already know." The second, delivered with enthusiastic admiration by a young person, "Dr. Shengold [my "occupation" restored, as Othello might say], what I like about your paper is that you have reminded us of what we already know." I think that they are both right, and I share some of the feeling of each.

---

8. I hope my readers will not tire of this word for the concept that I first heard spoken of by Anna Freud. It is the subject of my last chapter.

1

....

AN EXAMPLE
OF DELUSION
IN A
NEUROTIC
PERSON

Every normal person, in fact, is only normal on the
average. His ego approximates to that of the
psychotic in some part or other and to a
greater or lesser extent.
—Freud, *Analysis Terminable and Interminable*

There is no certain delineation of the development of the working
of the mind. One can view the mind in terms of archaic functioning (the way the infantile mind operates) that never disappears but
gradually becomes partially transformed into mature functioning
(the way the adult mind works)—see Lear 1990—with a development that features progressions, transformations, and regressions.
Freud contributed to our understanding with the distinction he
made between an early primitive kind of functioning, which he
called primary process thinking—that is later supplemented and
layered over by a more complex and reality centered kind of functioning, which he called secondary process thinking:

> We are driven to conclude that two fundamentally different
> kinds of psychical process are concerned in the formation of
> dreams. One of these [secondary process] produces perfectly
> rational dream thoughts, of no less validity than normal think-
> ing; while the other treats these thoughts in a manner which is in
> the highest degree bewildering and irrational [primary process].
> (Freud 1900, 597)

The dream is of course hallucinatory and is full of delusions—part
of archaic functioning that features what Freud called primary
process thinking. In the (usually mixed) metaphors of the early

and later Freudian pictures of the mind we encounter hypothetical places and structures (the unconscious; the id; the unconscious ego and superego) where primary process predominates, and those where secondary process is preponderant (the preconscious; the conscious parts of the ego and superego).

Freud thought of primary process and secondary process as working with different kinds of psychic energy: the primary with mobile or free energy that aims at discharge, the secondary with bound or inhibited energy that aims at establishing meaning. The mechanisms of the primary process are first and foremost displacement, condensation, and the disregarding of contradictions; loose, nonlogical associations (e.g., according to contiguity, sound); the transformation of thoughts into images (Freud 1900, 597). These conclusions were derived from Freud's thoughts on dreams, and the mechanisms are part of what he called the dream-work (unconscious, primary process distortions of preconscious, secondary process thoughts).

We all, neurotic and psychotic alike, retain (in individually varying qualities and intensities) a core of delusions and delusional feelings (for example, paranoid feelings) that stem from earliest psychic development. In the adult some of these partly transformed infantile remnants can be called quasi-delusions. Whether they are of full delusional or partly delusional quality, such residues of primitive thinking are instances of psychotic-like manifestations in everyone, including the mythical, statistically conceived "normal." This is neither a new nor an original idea, but its clinical relevance has been neglected. I believe I am describing something of what Freud refers to in the quote I have used as epigraph to this chapter.

I will give an example. A masochistic young woman whom I will call patient M had been in analysis for several years. She was married and was in the middle of a pregnancy. On this day she had arrived in my waiting room just as I had opened the door to my office. She strode in past me with an unusual air of determination and proceeded to lie down on the couch. She appeared to be very angry:

PATIENT. I am really pissed. [silence] I have to go to the obstetrician after this session. Again I've forgotten to bring a fasting urine sample. I've forgotten it the past three times. I knew I would forget it. I don't want to talk about this. I'm going to change the subject. I was angry [from her tone of voice I judged her to be still angry] because I wanted to go to the bathroom before the session. But your door was open, there you were, and I was embarrassed. It doesn't really matter though—unless *someone* [my italics] steps on my bladder.

ANALYST. The "change of subject" sounds more like a continuation. [I was the only someone around.]

PATIENT. I want to keep away from why I persist in forgetting the urine sample. I am furious at *his* nurse. I know that the test itself isn't important—I had a blood sugar done recently. *She* keeps talking about albumen. I always will forget. I guess I'm so angry because *she* gave me this short, narrow medical bottle to bring a sample in. It's impossible—no one could urinate into that bottle—at least no woman could.[1] I'm furious with *her* [these are the patient's emphases] and I'm damned if I am going to do it unless *she* gives me another kind of bottle. *It's just impossible to use that little thing* [my italics].

ANALYST. It sounds as if a few minutes of communication with the nurse could clear up the realistic part of the difficulty. Is

---

1. M equates "no one" with "woman." The vagina is "nothing" for her, as Lewin (1948) writes. M literally said, "The female genitals just amount to nothing." Note how M ends her speech: "It's just impossible to use that little thing." She is unconsciously talking about her clitoris.

there some need to be angry with the nurse and keep the feeling that she has done something to you?

PATIENT. The "impossibility" of using the bottle could be gotten over by getting another kind—or I could just use a funnel or a plastic cup and pour it into this bottle. But I just won't. It makes me so mad! If *she* wants that sample, *she* is going to have to solve the problem. [Sheepishly—the delusion fades.] I know how irrational all this is. The nurse is really a very nice person. I could easily talk to her about this or just bring in my own container. But I am really so furious about it that I put all my logic and knowledge aside and I feel stubborn—I just won't do it. *She* [back to the delusional emphasis] can't make me use that bottle. *She* gave it to me and it's up to *her* to solve the problem.

I will omit the circumstances that made it clear to me that the patient was dealing with a feeling of accusation toward her mother (psychologically, toward her "primal parent") transferred onto her analyst the doctor and then displaced onto the other doctor's nurse. I think the paranoid flavor of M's feelings is clearly brought out—the emphasis on "she" and "her" is the equivalent of what one hears (the music, not the words) in the paranoid's hated "They."

M's rational attitude toward what she was feeling and thinking about the nurse was also present in what I have quoted; but this, for the most part, was drowned out by the concomitant almost delusional, or perhaps fully delusional, conviction about being forced and deprived by someone hateful. The wish to continue to be so treated seemed to me to be obvious. This was a typical "stubborn" (M's own description) attitude—a kind of paranoid insistence that intermittently emanated from this predominantly passive, cooperative, sensible, and agreeable young woman—*suddenly* (I will return to the theme of "suddenly") giving her almost a different persona. There was a transient transformation to a hostile, provocative, spiteful, accusatory, unreasonable, willful child who seemed predominantly bent on taking a self-destructive, masochistic path with seeming disregard for the consequences. I sensed the shadow of an individually characteristic temper tantrum from M's childhood. She was, without having *responsible* knowledge of it, courting punishment and a repetition of a fantasied and actual traumatic past; this was present in the disguised form of the thought (unconscious wish) that the analyst would "step on [her] bladder." (*Responsible* is the key word in the understanding and clinical handling of this kind of phenomenon.) It was obvious to me that in a real way M knew what was going on in relation to the nurse and the urine sample bottle, but this kind of knowledge was for the time not being given access to her emotions, and she retained the sense of conviction that she would be persecuted (both a fear and a wish). To express this differently, there was alongside this ineffective and distanced "knowing" a much more powerful, unsynthesized "knowing" that at least approached delusional intensity. The depth of the delusional conviction wavered. When challenged, and even spontaneously, M could give lip service to the knowledge that she was breaking with reality, but this knowing was compartmentalized (split-off and isolated), transiently "sterile," as Freud said of the Rat Man in a similarly delusional situation:

> [The Rat Man] could not help believing in the premonitory power of dreams, for he had several remarkable experiences to prove it. Consciously he does not really believe in it. (The two views exist side by side, but the critical one is *sterile*). (1909, 268; my italics)

(Freud is describing a vertical split in the mind—a metaphor for the ability to contain two contradictory views simultaneously without any possibility of integrating them.)

These narcissistic delusions or quasi-delusions are often overlooked and minimized, and not only by patients. We neurotics all have them. They represent shards of primitive mental functioning, what Freud calls that "part" or "extent" of the ego (of the mind) "which resembles the psychotic" (1937, 235). They are compromise formations. The delusion fills a need to hold on both to gratifications and to defenses that stem from the early, narcissistic period of development. Both gratification and defense express narcissistic (or, to use Kohut's noun as an adjective, self-object) ways of connecting with or preserving the connections with a parent or a need-fulfilling part of a parent regarded as part of one's self.

In a previous pregnancy M had had a similar conviction (again, alongside some critically sterile knowing better) that she was growing a penis in her womb. Yes, she stated, this was a fantasy, "I *know* that." She said, after the baby was born, "Look, I knew perfectly well I was going to have a baby and that I was not growing a penis— but I still somehow believed it all the same, if you know what I mean."

I felt I did know what she meant, and some provisional and yet fixed superstitious or magical belief is common enough; many women have conscious quasi-delusions about having penises (see Calef and Weinshel 1981, 53). A diagnostically trendy critic of this book might say that M is "borderline" (a diagnostic category I find increasingly less useful). I would rejoin: If she is borderline, so are we all—in the specific sense that Freud described in 1937: "to a greater or lesser extent." Of course psychotics also have a range of intensity and extent in their delusions; one could say they have quasi-delusions alongside true delusions. The mind is a dynamic entity that provides a changing range of flexibilities and intensities. There are qualitative and quantitative varieties of all sorts of dynamic flows of feeling and idea that make for crucial diversities for and in every individual. When we are not dealing with obvious extremes, what have been characterized as borderline phenomena are not easily differentiated or discerned.

The symbolism of the "short," "little," and "narrow" implement associated with urination given by "*she*"/"*her*" (the mother/nurse defensively deprived of individuality) is, as I have noted, obvious. So is the evocation in the psychoanalyst of the complexes (preoedipal as well as oedipal) involving castration anxiety and penis envy. These complexes stem from the body, from the early body-ego; so does the basic metaphor (similarly derived from the primitive functioning and primal developmental period of the mind) involved in Freudian symbolization itself (see Shengold 1981). The emotional intensity that characterizes delusion and quasi-delusion, providing a stubborn, reductive, insistent, perfervid quality, marks a regression to the earliest, narcissistic, phase of psychic development during which the universe is regarded as comprised of the body and those parts and functions of others that are at first merged with and considered parts of one's own body. This early paradise-and-hell, bodily derived psychic cosmos provides the motive power for our function of symbolization as well as the material for "that which is symbolized." (In symbolizing, elements of the worlds outside the mind—body and external environment—are equated with elements of the world—bodily derived representations—within the mind. See Fliess 1973 and Appendix 1.) Narcissistic delusions or quasi-delusions mark the regressive return to, and the frequently transient but perceptible getting stuck in, a primitively functioning part of our unconscious minds (whether we are sick, normal, or healthy)—the part that remains under the sway of the early time of body ego dominance.[2] Narcissistic delusions are transformed derivations from, and sometimes a direct continuation of, our primal fantasies or fragments thereof, and they retain the power that those early bodily and drive-derived basic motivators possess to stretch and even break with later men-

2. Freud: "The ego is first and foremost a body ego" (1923, 26–27).

tal representations of external and internal reality.[3] It is a power full of magical promise and terrible dread.

It follows, of course, that these delusions and quasi-delusions are very difficult to analyze; they are frequently not conscious, existing as unconscious or at least not responsibly acknowledged assumptions and expectations and as associated affects (again, involving promise and dread) that are disconnected from responsible consciousness. And the delusions result in resistances to change in life and therefore give rise to stubborn resistances by the patient in therapy. In order to deal with the resistances, the analyst must recognize the delusional or near-delusional (remember, there is a spectrum here) qualities and convey these to the patient. Patients often have to struggle to see and especially to *own*, to become responsible for, these sometimes but not always subtle breaks with reality and reason. They often must learn (some already know) how much they want to hold on to the promise of intense gratification and the protection of powerful infantile defenses against intense bad feeling (together with the ties to the godlike parents of infancy, with whom these feelings are so implicated). I may be saying what many already know, but it is my impression that the

3. These fantasies are also influenced by external reality, and M was in fact a victim of sexual abuse as a child. She was first seduced to performing fellatio by an adult relative who was *urinating* when she *opened the door* and walked in on him *in the bathroom. Suddenly* (I am emphasizing elements corresponding to the clinical material I have presented), in the course of the seduction (as the child passed from initial pleasurable excitement to overstimulation), the man changed for her from his usual benignity to a terrifying, abusive, uncontrollable monster. I have written of this elsewhere (see Shengold 1978, 1989) and have specifically described (1989) an "and suddenly" reaction that I have often seen in victims of child abuse based on the sudden transformation of the adult in the child's perceptions (and probably also in reality) from one who promises pleasure and love to the hating and hated tormentor.

current general diagnostic fervor, what might be called DSM-mania (no human being can be reduced to a diagnosis), and the specific fashion for borderline diagnosis have distanced many from acceptance of the wise and cautionary insight of Freud with which I opened this chapter.

2

. . . .

NARCISSISTIC

DELUSIONS

> . . . for within the hollow crown
> That rounds the mortal temples of a king
> Keeps Death his court, and there the antic sits,
> Scoffing his state, and grinning at his pomp;
> Allowing him a breath, a little scene,
> To monarchize, be fear'd, and kill with looks,
> *Infusing him with self and vain conceit,*
> *As if this flesh which wall about our life*
> *Were brass impregnable;* and humour'd thus
> Comes at the last and with a little pin
> Bores through his castle wall, and—farewell king!
> —Shakespeare, *Richard II* (my italics)

Narcissism refers to the time of the infant's dawning mental development, when there is little differentiation of oneself from the parent and the external world—when, subjectively, there are no others and even, perhaps, no subjectivity. (I am, throughout this paragraph, stating as fact what is based on theory.) Although narcissistic manifestations continue throughout life, narcissism starts too far back for memory to reach: in the infant's first few months of life, when inner registrations of the external world begin to occur, forming congealing islands of ego development. These primal mental events are derived from feelings stemming from the body (only partially separated in the infantile mind from parts of the parental body). They would be the beginnings of emotions and thoughts: perceptions and sensations developing into protoemotions and protothoughts. These early somatically charged mental manifestations would lie, to reverse Wordsworth's well-known lines, too deep for thoughts.[1]

Whatever the infant's mentation (which no adult can remember), it would likely be partly in the form of hallucination and delusion. Only speculations and precarious inferences based on the observation of children can guide one here, in the time of the unrememberable, the preverbal, personal prehistoric, primal period of psychic life. We cannot know how much mind the infant possesses at birth. We must gather evidence of this early time from palimpsest-like later impressions of primitive mental functioning that, consequent to further development (of ego apparatus), have attained some memory status.

Another way of putting this: narcissism is personal, "prehistoric" myth: the disguised, reworked remnants of our earliest mental registrations patched together (or patchable together) in the course of development into narrative. Like all myths that survive and become communicable, there is some retention from beginning versions, but the narrative undergoes a constant transformational process—additions and distortions that suit the needs of each progressive (historical or personal) period of development; the dynamics are complicated by regressive manifestations within each period. There are needs to express something, based on our instinctual drives and acquired exigencies; and needs to suppress something, based on our basic defensive requirements. We go toward pleasure and away from pain. Shared cultural myths evolve in ways similar to the personal myths they express. It is therefore appropriate to start the examination of narcissistic myths with the myth of Narcissus.

1. Tears (or their somatic-emotional counterparts) that lie too deep for thoughts, instead of "Thoughts that do often lie too deep for tears" (1807, 590).

If we desire to follow a historical path in our research (in any research into the preverbal and prehistoric), we can start only *toward,* not at, the actual beginning. Alternatively, we can begin (as with any recurrent narrative recounted in a clinical situation) with present versions and work toward abstracting backward to earlier ones, although probably never arriving at genesis.

The current version of the myth of Narcissus would be a composite that, I assume, retains something of the original. Here is the information given under the heading "Narcissus" in a fairly recent edition, for American readers, of Webster's dictionary (the literary equivalent, in respect to potential analyzability, of a recital of a story about the past by an American adult):

> *Narcissus.* In Greek mythology, a beautiful youth for unrequited love of whom Echo died. Nemesis in punishment caused him to pine away for love of his own reflection in a spring and changed him into the narcissus [flower]. (1953, 975)

The first preserved written account of Narcissus is from Ovid, whose *Metamorphoses* dates from about A.D. 10. Ovid has Narcissus courted by both men and women. But it is only the image of himself in a fountain that he can love. To love oneself is (or, better, appears to be) essentially a homosexual love. Narcissus addresses the young man in the water:

> Hear, gentle youth, and pity my complaint,
> Come from thy well, thou fair inhabitant.
> My charms an easy conquest have obtain'd
> O'er other hearts, by thee alone disdain'd.
> But why should I despair? I'm sure he burns
> With equal flames, and languishes by turns. (Ovid A.D. 10, 86)[2]

2. This is love that cannot be requited accompanied by a delusional insistence that it can—an essential characteristic of narcissistic love. Readers of Proust will recognize its qualities. It can appear to be homosexual, as with Narcissus (Proust

According to Ovid, Teiresias, who through divine enchantment had been both man and woman, told Narcissus's mother, Leiriope, "Narcissus will live to a ripe old age, provided he never knows himself" (Graves 1955, 286). (Teiresias was the same blind prophet whom Oedipus would not listen to; Leiriope's was his first consultation, and it gained him fame perhaps in part because it was, slyly, both misleading and true.) Echo, a nymph who never dies (contra Webster), although she fades away and is reduced to her sonic mirroring iteration, is, in Ovid's account, present as a spectator at the death of Narcissus. Narcissus addresses his reflection:

> "Ah Youth! belov'd in vain," Narcissus cries;
> "Ah Youth! belov'd in vain," the nymph replies.
> "Farewel," says he; the parting sound scarce fell
>   From his faint lips, but she reply'd, "farewel." (286)

(Echo would appear to be portrayed here as a feminine, mother derived "reflection" of Narcissus—the afterimage of his mirrored self.) Narcissus's mother, the nymph Leiriope,[3] is said to be the nymph of the spring in which Narcissus gets entrapped by his reflection (see Henseler 1991, 208). I cannot find the source for this, but it is of course in the reflection of the admiring eye of the

---

defines homosexual love in this way), or heterosexual (Swann and Odette in Proust)—but its genetic basis lies in the period of bisexual potential that comes before true sexual differentiation, when the infant wants sexually to be and to have everything.

3. Leiriope's name literally means "lily face" (Graves 1955, 398), and this too contributes to the meaning of her eyes as the pool or spring in which Narcissus sees himself. Henseler says, "He is reflected in the water of the spring whose nymph is his mother, Leiriope" (1991, 208). Bela Grünberger, in his book on narcissism (1971), relates Narcissus's fascinated entrapment in water to his wish to return to amniotic fluid. (I am indebted to Leonard B. Klein for directing me to Henseler and Grünberger.)

mother (or the delusion thereof) that our narcissism begins and in which the narcissist gets caught.[4]

In Pausanius's account (second century A.D.), Narcissus was punished not because he spurned Echo but for sending "a sword to Ameinus, his most insistent suitor, after whom the river Ameinus is named. . . . Ameinus killed himself on Narcissus's threshold, calling on the gods to avenge his death" (Graves, 287). And Artemis (perhaps in remorse for having similarly been murderous toward Acteon, who lusted after her?) responds and sends Narcissus to his fate. In other renderings later than Ovid, Narcissus stabs himself (talion punishment for Ameinus's death) rather than pining away.

In all these readings, there lurk promises and dangers: magic (for good and for evil), immortality (and getting stuck forever), eternal youth (and complete loss of identity), transcendence of sexual need for others (and consequent punishment by fate), bisexual fulfillment (and the dangers of death and castration). Here is the stuff of narcissistic delusion.

The ingenious Robert Graves, innocent of any psychoanalytic

---

4. By his transformation into the flower, narcissus, the youth is made immortal and, according to Ovid, unchanging. (It is ironic that the narcissus, although a hardy perennial, is a delicate and transient flower and yet has the significance here of unchangeability. This accords well with delusional personal myth linking the transiency of infancy with immortality that denies change). Ovid writes,

To the cold shades his flitting ghost retires,
And in the Stygian wave itself admires. (10, 88)

The name of the flower is derived from the Greek *narke*, which means stupor—apparently in relation to the *narcotic* effect of the oil that can be abstracted from the flower. Narcotic addiction involves a regression to or fixation on the early narcissistic period of psychic development. Drugs can promise and transiently grant the illusion of the fulfillment of delusional wishes for omnipotence and immortality. (So can sexual ecstasy and other more tranquil transcendent experiences.)

point of view, connects the Narcissus myth with an early Greek icon that shows one of two mythical matricides—Alcmaeon or Orestes:

> lying crowned with lilies beside a pool in which he has vainly tried to purify himself after murdering his mother. . . . Echo, in this icon, would represent the mocking ghost of his mother, and Ameinus his murdered father. (1955, 288)

The unrequited sexual longing by the suitors in the myth would then represent those of the mother and father for the son, Narcissus, reflecting the reversal that characterizes the sexual component of the Oedipus complex in later life. Incestuous and murderous desires for the parent in childhood and early youth begin increasingly, in the course of an individual's subsequent adult development, to become directed toward the child, alongside retention of the original focus on the parent. The child would also be a reflection of the parent's (the adult's) *quondam* self; this provides another psychoanalytic layer of meaning that Freud brings to the Narcissus myth: the vain search for one's former self in a (narcissistic) love object. This unfulfillable quest is the source of so much unhappiness for both narcissistic homosexuals and heterosexuals—and to some extent for all of us, since we are all in varying degree narcissistic. We must, in order to love another, be able to settle for less than finding our own perfect self-image or its sometimes hidden but always present counterpart, the perfect parental image. (Either or both can be the unconscious source for love objects.)

Part of the delusional matrix of narcissism that makes for reluctance to mature is the aura of Promise (it should be capitalized)—the future of bliss guaranteed by the godlike parent who can spare the child every change, loss, pain, and danger and who grants immortality and omnipotence. Thus, in Sophocles' play, Jocasta runs away when she realizes, before Oedipus does, what the old shepherd is about to reveal to him: that she, now Oedipus's wife, gave the infant Oedipus over to be killed and so is not only also his mother but a mother who was capable of murderous rejection. Poor narcissistic Oedipus dismisses Jocasta's desertion as motivated by her reluctance to learn that she has married someone who might have been a slave. Let the proud woman go and bear her shame, he says; he doesn't care how lowly his race is, since: "I, who hold myself son of Fortune that gives good, will not be dishonoured. She [Fortune] is the mother from whom I spring" (Sophocles, 165).

Oedipus thus tries to protect himself, by using the primary, narcissistic defenses of minimization, idealization, and denial, from the mortification of knowing that he had been both the object of his mother's murderous impulse and guilty with her of the crime of incest. He tries, by using denial, to ward off the attendant primal dangers of loss of the mother and castration. Ironically, this defensive insistence on having a goddesslike mother, so full of hubris, comes just as Fortune (as bad a mother as was the Jocasta who gave him over as a crippled infant to be abandoned and left to die) is about to reveal to him his terrible crimes and his fate—the revelation that will lead to his blinding himself. The intensity of narcissistic promise (the *idealization* that stems from our earliest mental existence), which seems so loving and sexual, is matched and often overmatched by the intensity of narcissistic dangers, so intertwined with aggression and hatred. (These dangers inherent to destructive impulse are present in the earliest use of *devaluation*, the other face of idealization. I view these as primal defensive modes, operating through the early psychic defense mechanisms of projection and introjection [Shengold 1990].) The self-hatred becomes the need for punishment.

Because we all retain a considerable degree of narcissism, "alongside and beneath" later developments, it follows that we all have some degree and variety of narcissistic delusion. A delusion is, according to Webster, "in psychiatry, a false, persistent belief not substantiated by sensory evidence" (1953, 389). (To make this a more satisfactory definition one should emphasize the "persistent" and add the tremendous emotional intensity that characterizes the conviction in the "belief.") There is a most complicated spectrum of delusion, ranging from psychotic delusions, in which almost no doubt in the belief is allowed; through delusions in which the reality can be given lip service without disturbing the false belief, as if these were in two different compartments of the mind which cannot connect (I have called these quasi-delusions);[5] to transient insistent beliefs in which conviction and doubt are both present, one alongside the other, yet able to intermix, as it were, without canceling one another out. Each individual would have his own dynamic stock and variety (all along the spectrum) of narcissistic delusions, even including what might be called psychotic ones. The differences between the so-called normal (that is, the neurotic) and the psychotic individual are probably mostly quantitative, having to do with preponderances, although the latter can be present in such measure as to present the effect of qualitative diversity, and also there can be true qualitative differences having to do with specific delusional content and related emotions and impulses.

For example, past early childhood most of us who are not psychotic cannot but accept the reality of death as it is forced upon us by the conditions of our existence. Because none of us but the dying can have the experience, the acceptance is ordinarily more than intellectual but less than experiential, and never complete. And we all retain differing degrees of delusional claim to personal exemption from what we also know is the universal fate.

5. Ego alterations that refer to sometimes more or less permanent, sometimes intermittent erasure of secondary process functioning in specific areas.

Freud recognized that it requires the experience and development of an adult to appreciate the reality of death: "To children, who, moreover, are spared the sight of the scenes of suffering which precede death, being 'dead' means approximately the same as being 'gone'—not troubling the survivors any longer. A child makes no distinction as to how this absence is brought about: whether it is due to a journey, to a dismissal, to an estrangement, or to death" (1900, 254–55).

Adult awareness is always subject to regression to the child's underlying delusionary denial of death. Freud, in a 1919 note added to the Dream book, documented one step in the modification of the delusion of a very young child:

> An observation made by a person who had a knowledge of psycho-analysis caught the actual moment at which his highly intelligent four-year-old daughter perceived the distinction between being "gone" and being "dead."

This distinction, the acquisition of which marks the girl as on the road to becoming an adult, covers over the retained delusion of immortality.

> The little girl had been troublesome at meal-time and noticed that one of the maids at the pension where they were staying was looking at her askance. "I wish Josefine was dead," was the child's comment to her father. "Why dead?" enquired her father soothingly; "wouldn't it do if she went away?" "No," replied the child; "then she'd come back again." The unbounded self-love (the narcissism) of children regards any interference as an act of *lèse majesté*; and their feelings demand (like the Draconian code) that any such crime shall receive the one form of punishment which admits of no degrees. (1900, 254)

This modification involves the death of an unwanted other (part of the murderous intensity of preoedipal and oedipal rivalry with one competed-with parent for the other, and of siblings for both parents). Note that the child cannot easily come to terms with the death of a parent felt as wanted or needed, or of the child's self. There denial still reigns—to be stirred up when illness or accident threatens or occurs. The denial of death is not usually apparent at the surface of the adult's mind, but the child is there beneath the surface.

The assumption that one will never die, lying in the depths of the psyche, is perhaps the most familiar narcissistic delusion. Here is Tolstoy writing of the reaction of an ordinary man to his fatal illness. Ivan Ilyich, John, son of Eli, is a sort of Russian John Doe, no more or less narcissistic than the average man:

> Ivan Ilyich saw that he was going to die, and he was in perpetual despair. In the depths of his soul, he knew that he was going to die; but he not only failed to get used to the thought, but also simply did not comprehend it, could not comprehend it.

Tolstoy here portrays the vertical split in consciousness, the part that knows alongside the part that refuses to know, which so often goes along with, and sometimes disguises, delusion.

> This form of syllogism, which he had studied in Kiziveter's "Logic"—"Kai is a man, men are mortal, therefore Kai is mortal"—had seemed to him all his life true only in its application to Kai, but never to himself. It was Kai as man, as man in general, and in this respect it was perfectly correct; but he was not Kai, and not man in general, and he had always been an entity absolutely, absolutely distinct from all others; he had been Vanya with mamma and papa, with Mitya and Volodya, with his playmates, the coachman, with the nurse . . . with all the joys, sorrows, enthusiasms of childhood, boyhood, youth.

[To try to ensure his immortality, Ivan Ilyich thinks back to his childhood with mamma and papa when, as Vanya (little Ivan), he

innocently, consciously, automatically assumed he would live forever.]

> Was it Kai who smelt the odor of the little striped leather ball
> that Vanya had loved so dearly? Was it Kai who had kissed his
> mother's hand?; and was it for Kai that the silken folds of his
> mother's dress had rustled so pleasantly? . . . "And Kai is certainly
> mortal, and it is proper that he should die; but for me, Vanya,
> Ivan Ilyich, with all my feelings, my thoughts,—for me, that is
> another thing, and it cannot be that I must take my turn and die.
> That would be too horrible. . . . If I were going to die like Kai,
> then, surely, I should have known it; some internal voice would
> have told me; but nothing of the sort happened in me, and I
> myself, and my friends, all of us, have perceived that it was
> absolutely different in our case from what it was with Kai. But
> now how is it?" he said to himself. "It cannot be, it cannot be,
> but it is! How is this? How to understand it?" And he could not
> understand it. (Tolstoy 1886, 394)

Understanding of an experiential kind could reduce the delusion,
but Tolstoy cannot adequately understand it any more than any of
us can. He can approach the roots of understanding and give us
perspective—Ivan Ilyich connecting the present with the past begins to do this, but in an inadequate and heartbreaking way. He has
for the most part lived his life unthinkingly, distancing mortality,
and it is only in the moments before dying that he becomes truly
human. His awareness that he is dying had at first enhanced his
narcissism; he could think of others, even his children, only with
indifference or envy. In the story, the actual approach to death does
restore his ability to love and perhaps even amplifies it. Before the
change that takes place just as Ivan is dying there is a transfigura-
tion, some sort of marvelous luminosity and merger with the universe that perhaps approximates the primal narcissistic promise of

infancy. The point of Tolstoy's great story is that the only way to transcend death is not through understanding it but by experiencing it. For those who are not dying, it is being able to remember (memento mori!) and accept the idea and reality of death that can grant the most profound perspective of which humans are capable. "Death kills a man, but the idea of death saves him," says E. M. Forster. Transience can enhance value and love.

Vladimir Nabokov, in his autobiography, links his capacity for personal love with his need for immortality, beautifully condensing an expression of his disdain for the conditions of life evoked by the unbearable loss of the object of one's love and the poignancy of the idea of a stop to one's consciousness and memory: "Whenever I start thinking of my love for a person, I am in the habit of immediately drawing radii from my love—from my heart, from the tender nucleus of a personal matter—to monstrously remote points of the universe. . . . I have to have all space and all time participate in my emotion, in my mortal love, so that the edge of its mortality is taken off, thus helping me to fight the utter degradation, ridicule, and horror of having developed an infinity of sensation and thought within a finite existence" (1966, 296–97).[6]

I was once seeing in psychoanalytic treatment two middle-aged physicians whose denial of death transcended the usual bounds. The denial pervaded despite more frequent daily experiences with the dying and the dead than most people have. One was a psychiatrist, A, who had sought out that branch of medicine to minimize contact with the body, blood, and death. Although death was inev-

6. Boyd, Nabokov's biographer, comments on this quotation: "This states the problem Nabokov addresses throughout his art: what can we make of the breach between the limitless capacity of consciousness and its absurd limitation? To answer this, he has searched relentlessly for some consciousness beyond the boundaries of the human" (1990, 10).

itably thrust upon him by the narrated experiences of his patients, he was able, transiently, to treat the people and the events as hypothetical; what he was hearing became part of a story that had "as if" quality. Once, when a particular patient's child died, A could distantly appreciate the terrible emotional loss involved, but essentially he became guiltily annoyed with the bereaved parent and abstracted away from any true empathy. That his old parents might die was unthinkable. As they advanced through their seventies, toward eighty, the age that marked being "really old" was pushed ahead. He could not help being angry with them or with his wife and children if any of them became ill. Intimations of mortality were intolerable. Yet he had become a physician. Like Ivan Ilyich, he would, when confronted by limitations that connoted mortality, try to reassure himself by recalling specific sensory details from his early childhood or reciting family sayings that had been preserved by endless repetition. He would call or visit his parents. He would return to childlike habits, indulge in hobbies that stemmed from his early life—in general, think and act in a childish manner that had its charm as well as pathos and contained occasional selfishness and cruelty, since he was shutting away his present life and companions. In analysis, he would willfully, often petulantly, if my comments or his own associations brought out mortal implications and/or murderous anger, announce, "I am now transforming myself into a child." This would, in effect, make me disappear as a meaningful other person. (Narcissism is usually the enemy of love.)

The other death-denying doctor, B, had paradoxically become a pathologist. But there was little or no appreciation that the corpses over whom he labored had been human beings with lives and personalities. They were "as if" people for him. Lewin (1946) has pointed out that, in medical training, the student's first "patient" is a cadaver, completely passive and requiring no empathy. He believes that the consequence of this can be the tendency for physicians to treat patients not as human beings but as anonymous anatomical models who are carriers of disease: they are different from us. This dehumanization establishes an emotional distance, comfortable and convenient for some physicians—perhaps even necessary for surgeons, at least while they are operating; of course the patient is deprived of the sympathetic contact that can provide an important predisposition toward healing. R. Fliess, in a paper (1954) entitled "The Autopsic Encumbrance," applied Lewin's observation to the psychoanalyst, whose patient, supine on the couch, can unconsciously evoke the cadaver when the analyst becomes emotionally threatened by his or her inner resonances with the analysand's associations. The analyst can also mirror the patient's resistant silences, blanknesses, and inactivity. (These manifestations would be countertransference in its original sense: that aspect of the analyst's reaction to the patient that interferes with the analyst's functioning.) Dr. B felt no danger from emotional involvements until he began to connect, when associating on the couch (and against the greatest resistance), his dead "patients" with meaningful people—people who could come alive in his mind —from his past and present. He had many acquaintances but no real friends because any depth of feeling threatened loss. He was in a perpetual state of frustrated exasperation with his parents. Nothing they could do for him could possibly approach the intensity of his need to sustain his narcissistic delusions.

Dr. B's conscious preoccupations featured denial of his parents', especially of his mother's, mortality more than denial of his own. For the most part, his mother (and at first his analyst) was perfect. About me, on whom he had transferred his mother (or perhaps projected her as part of himself would be more accurate), he said,

> I know that the mystical, ideal feelings I have about you as perfect are crazy—my brain tells me that. It's all there for me: the idea that you will never get old, that I will always have you. But

my heart tells me it is true all the same. Only at moments do I see you as a separate real person and that I am not under your control nor you under mine.

But this kind of delusional conviction of the other's perfection was much harder to maintain about his mother, for long since she was subject to recurrent irrational rages. He could watch her direct these at other people, especially strangers, with relative equanimity, but they were repetitively also aimed at him in the form of vicious verbal assaults. It was difficult to treat such attacks, and the counterrages they evoked in the patient, as not having happened, but after a while Dr. B was able to manage it. His mind was divided into nonconnecting compartments, vertical splits which could contain completely separate, contradictory ideas, feelings, and ways of functioning. For much of the time this form of maintaining delusion and idealization ("my perfect mommy") could work because he allowed no integration. After one vituperative, recriminatory outburst attributed (as was frequent) by his mother to her son's neglect of her, he reported,

For a while I was in a rage with her. I still am, I suppose. But I can't bear it. [He begins to cry.] When I get that angry I feel that mother is dead; dead!

[This is the delusional mode and intensity.]

But if I think about it, when I can think about it, I suppose it means that in my rage I feel that it is as if my mother could die, that I could really lose her.

[Here the delusional quality begins to fade; the infant is becoming an adult again, an adult who can at least hypothetically accept death and loss.]

But, you know, that last thought, that "as if," is intellectual. And I begin to get frightened when I feel she really could die. Don't you understand? She really could. I just refuse to accept it!

So the delusion, or quasi-delusion, returns. Following the session it sets in beneath the surface, the as-if surface, where what appears to be the predominantly adult functioning of Dr. B can fool not only the observer but, above all, Dr. B himself.

Both Dr. A and Dr. B had been spoiled as children by frightened and overindulgent parents who had difficulty refusing their children anything. In the psychic universe transmitted by these dependent and childlike parents to their sons, any "no" was equated with death, the great negation of life, and so "no" became intolerable, evoking terror and rage. Instead, the world these parents helped construct for their children was full of the Promise, that unfulfillable, false promise, of continual narcissistic bliss. Both boys, as they grew up and were inevitably[7] exposed to the insistent demands of the external world and the terrifying dangers attendant on their own unchecked instinctual wishes, needed to cling desperately to the delusion of their own and their parents' power and immortality. To lose the idealized self-image mirrored in the parental eyes (Narcissus gazing at his reflection in the spring) was and remained an unbearable loss that could be denied only by delusion. Whenever this delusion was challenged, there arose a dreadful, intense rage—paradoxically, a *murderous* rage directed toward the indispensable parents and their false promises; this of course only intensified the danger of loss. The rage was ineffectually expressed in tantrums, which the parents found intolerable and usually tried to smother with indulgence rather than handle with discipline. The child (mirroring the childlike parents) was in the trap that all of us are caught in to some extent: the urge to kill those one cannot live without. But the intensity of their entrapment,

---

7. Dr. B once said, "The two words I hate most are 'inevitable' and 'inexorable'."

appropriate to early infancy, had, disguised and sequestered, been fully retained in adult life. Most of us are able to modify (but never to eliminate) the vicious cycle—a modification that can be lost regressively if the conditions of life make old dangers return.

Accompanying the delusion of immortality is the delusion of omnipotence.[8] When threatened or offended, patient C would resort to a fantasy of transforming himself into a Greek god. Although this also had the connotation for him of being infinitely handsome and lovable (another quasi-delusional belief), it was the god's magical power to command changes in reality, especially to get rid of people who were obstacles to his wishes and whims, that he was calling upon. He thought of himself as Zeus or Poseidon (or Jupiter or Neptune—the Romans, having defeated the Greeks, made these the preferred names) wielding thunderbolts. All this was voiced in a manner that usually sounded jovial enough, but the intensity of need underlying the appearance of playfulness frequently showed through in an isolated, near hysterical tone; more rarely he would say, directly and convincingly, "I really mean this!" —again, with an obvious split in conscious awareness. (This kind of split was described by Freud in a note added to *The Interpretation of Dreams* in 1909: "I was astonished to hear a highly intelligent boy of ten remark after the sudden death of his father: 'I know father's dead, but what I can't understand is why he doesn't come home to supper'" [1900, 254].)

8. See the important ideas and confirming clinical material in Novick and Novick's paper (1991) on the delusion of omnipotence. They disagree with my (and I would think most analysts') assumption that omnipotence is present at (or soon after) the beginning of mental life; instead they see it as a defensive phenomenon (which it certainly also is), especially in relation to masochistic patients. What I share with the Novicks is the clear impression that "this fantasy [of omnipotence] constitutes a major component of the resistance so prominent in work with masochistic patients" (307). I would add that the regression to narcissism and omnipotence is found, in different varieties and degrees, in all human beings.

As a child, C's claim to the assumption of godlike power had been admired and, apparently, even acceded to whenever possible by his parents, especially his father. But this had frightened C; the son required his father to keep the godlike power in order to protect him if his own magic failed. This unresolvable dilemma complicated C's oedipal development: taking his father's place and powers was at once too easy (not made less so by a seductive mother) and too terrifying. One way this conflicted godlike claim showed itself in his current life was that C, a prosperous businessman, repeatedly allowed his now almost indigent father to pay for the meals they frequently had together in expensive restaurants. The knowledge that the father couldn't afford the expense was put aside by both parties in deference to their mutual need to maintain the delusion of infinite parental resources with which the father could endow the son. There must be no limit, no contravening of the child's desires. This made for a powerful, entrapping bond between parent and child that had many levels of meaning and served to distance as well as to preserve the terrifying, murderous implications for both.

A concomitant delusional aspect of omnipotence and immortality is the claim to perfection, most often felt as intolerance for any defect, limitation, contingency, or postponement. For Dr. B, the pathologist whose relations with people were so unsatisfactory and superficial—other people were always, he felt, disappointing him—perfection was in the realm of things. Only with things could complete control be at least approached. He was a model of anal defensiveness: fastidious in his dress and appearance, a collector and putter of things in order, a classifier and labeler. Things, as lifeless as the cadavers he dissected, were, in his view, the least likely to age or change.

I am not trying to present an inclusive list, but I will mention one other basic delusion inherent to narcissism that is usually preconscious: the conviction that no one really counts outside the family—a continuation of the primal family as the universe, an assumption that fades for most of us but never disappears. This is part of the human condition—the easy disbelief in the separate existence of other human beings besides the self and the inner registration of one's parents. For some it holds, at least intermittently, much of its original power. Patient D led a good part of her emotional life in her original universe. Her parents dominated her existence; her husband, and to a lesser extent her son (who, in a repetition of D's childhood, had been alternately turned over completely to a housekeeper or clung to symbiotically), had a lesser, largely "as if" significance. This could change quickly in danger situations, such as separation and loss, in which husband and child would attain for D the central narcissistic parental exigent indispensability. Enrolling her three-year-old son in nursery school made D acutely anxious:

> I feel a child should never leave the parent. That's the way it should be. It sounds mad when I say it. But there is some way I really believe it. I feel that letting my son go to school will mean that something sexual will happen to him—that they are interested in accepting him because they are interested in his body.

D had some dim realization that she was projecting her past onto her son, but this did not affect the depth of her delusive expectations.

She was able, after postponements, interfering parapraxes, and much anguish, to force herself to let her (usually passive) husband take the active role in supervising the enrollment procedure.

A specific concomitant: for D (and for many others too) all sex really belonged in the family; sex meant incest. At this point such an assumption was beyond her responsible awareness. She simply said, "Not being able to let my son go is part of my strongest persuasions. I have never been able to face leaving my mother. Who besides Mother could take care of me if I got sick?" Indeed, both sets of parents had bought and furnished this couple's home and were in constant attendance to fulfill their every need, and for D unconsciously this meant sexual need too.

To return to the delusion of immortality: it is challenged by the danger of aging (as in the Norse myth of Iduna and the apples and its reflection in Freia in Wagner's *Das Rheingold*). Without eternal youth, living forever can be disgusting and terrible. Jonathan Swift illustrates this with the race of Struldbruggs, in Gulliver's voyage to Luggnagg—one of the parts of *Gulliver's Travels* that has little appeal for children. Among the Luggnaggians, there are rare births of a child "with a red circular spot in the forehead, directly over the left eyebrow, which was an infallible mark that it should never die" (1726, 121). On hearing of these immortals, Gulliver is full of admiration and envy; he wants to meet and would like to be one of these wonderful creatures who would have the time to gain both wisdom and power and therefore be in the way of doing much good for ordinary humans. They would be like a race of gods, making wonderful discoveries, spreading civilization, finding out the secrets of perpetual health. If he were to become one of them, "I should then see the discovery of the longitude, the perpetual motion, the universal medicine, and many other great inventions, brought to the utmost perfection" (123).

He and they could

communicate [their] observations and memories through the course of time, remark the several gradations by which corruption steals into the world, and oppose it in every step by giving perpetual warning and instruction to mankind, which, added to the strong influence of their own example, would probably prevent that continual degeneracy of human nature so justly complained of in all ages. (129)

Gulliver's envy is narcissistic in that he wants immortality, wealth, wisdom, and power for himself, but it is an idealized narcissism that is to be benevolently transformed to the purpose of benefiting others (see chapter 3). The Luggnaggians laugh at his responses. His interpreter, who had been an ambassador abroad, tells Gulliver that

> the system of living contrived by [him] was unreasonable and unjust, because it supposed a perpetuity of youth, health, and vigour, which no man could be so foolish to hope, however extravagant he may be in his wishes. That the question therefore was not whether a man would choose to be always in the prime of youth, attended with prosperity and health, but how he would pass a perpetual life under all the usual disadvantages which old age brings along with it. For although few men will avow their desires of being immortal upon such hard conditions, yet in the two kingdoms . . . of Balnibarbi and Japan, he observed that every man desired to put off death for some time longer, let it approach ever so late; and he rarely heard of any man who died willingly, except he were incited by the extremity of grief or torture. . . . Only in this island of Luggnagg the appetite for living was not so eager, from the continual example of the Struld-bruggs before their eyes. (123–24)

Swift here, as in all the voyages of Gulliver, is satirizing life as he knows it in England and Ireland. The Struldbruggs are the very old with their defects, many stemming from the regressive narcissism of second childhood made monstrous by their immortality.

Gulliver is further told:

> When [the Struldbruggs] came to fourscore years, which is reck-oned the extremity of living in this country, they had not only all the follies and infirmities of other old men, but many more

which arose from the dreadful prospect of never dying. They were not only opinionative, peevish, covetous, morose, vain, talkative, but uncapable of friendship, and dead to all natural affection, which never descended below their grandchildren. Envy and impotent desires are their prevailing passions. . . . They have no remembrance of anything but what they learned and observed in their youth and middle age, and even that is very imperfect. . . . The least miserable among them appear to be those who turn to dotage, and entirely lose their memories. (124)

Ironically, Swift was describing his own future terrible last years of madness and misanthropy. *Gulliver's Travels* was published in 1726, when Swift was fifty-nine and at the height of his powers. In words almost specifically prophetic of his own fate he describes the Struldbruggs as

[losing] their teeth and hair, they have . . . no distinction of taste, but eat and drink whatever they can get, without relish or appetite. The diseases they were subject to still continue without increasing or diminishing. In talking they forget the common appellation of things, and the names of persons, even of those who are their nearest friends and relations. For the same reason they never can amuse themselves with reading, because their memory will not serve to carry them from the beginning of a sentence to the end; and by this defect they are deprived of the only entertainment whereof they might otherwise be capable. (125)

Swift ended, during his last four or five years, in what a biographer (the son and namesake of Swift's good friend Thomas Sheridan and father of the playwright Richard Sheridan) who knew him calls a "fit of lunacy which continued some months, and then he sunk into a state of idiocy, which lasted to his death" (Sheridan

1747?, lxxxii). In 1736, when Swift was almost seventy, four years
before the fit of lunacy,

> his memory was greatly impaired, and his other faculties of
> imagination and intellect decayed, in proportion as the stores
> from which they were supplied diminished. When the under-
> standing was shaken from its seat, and reason had given up the
> reins, the irascible passions which at all times he had found
> difficult to be kept within due bounds, now raged without con-
> trol, and made him a torment to himself, and to all who were
> about him. An unusually long fit of deafness, attended with
> giddiness[9] which lasted almost a year, had disqualified him
> wholly from conversation, and made him lose all relish for so-
> ciety. Conscious of his situation he was little desirous of seeing
> any of his friends and companions, and they were as little solic-
> itous to visit him in that deplorable state. He could now no
> longer amuse himself with writing; and a resolution he had
> formed of never wearing spectacles, to which he obstinately
> adhered, prevented him from reading. Without employment,
> without amusements of any sort, thus did his time pass heavily
> along. (xxxi)

Swift died nine years later, ending as a Struldbrugg. Even years
before the onset of his overwhelming disabilities, Swift suffered
from dread that he would outlive his intellect. He had once told a
friend who came upon him staring at a tree whose head had been
blasted, "I shall be like that tree, I shall die first at the top" (lxxxi).

What is the importance of stressing what most clinicians are so
familiar with? Analyzing narcissism is part of every psychoanalysis.
Narcissistic delusional wishes and needs are brought to every authority figure, every parental substitute. The analyst sooner or

---

9. Twentieth-century physicians have concluded that Swift suffered from Mé-
nière's syndrome.

later—unless the patient runs away—is invested with the magical mythical powers of the early parent. We are constantly beset by the temptation of seeking magical solutions, involuntarily regressing with great ease to hope and sometimes insistence that primal parental magic can be acquired and assimilated. We know this—it is easy to know about others. About ourselves there is the split awareness which allows for personal exemption from limitations—a split which is a remnant of the primitive defenses of the narcissistic period, when contradictions could be left unresolved.

What is specifically important to those who try to modify, heal, and expand the minds of others is that narcissistic delusions must first be recognized in order to be deprived of their magical intensity. Only if the delusion is deprived of much of its emotional power can a relatively stable psychic change come about. Such change, when brought about by analysis, is based on insight derived from the patient's becoming able to work with and modify feelings, defenses, and impulses which come to be centered on the analyst, with transference. Working out this insight decreases infantile dependence on the parent and the parental substitute—now no longer felt as the only one who can sustain one's emotional life (like Narcissus's mirrored image). It is necessary to give up much of one's narcissistic claim in order to be able to love, to care about and care for another *separate* human being. If the capacity for caring remains narcissistic, either to the pitch of not recognizing the other except as an extension of oneself (or to the lesser extent of remaining dependent on the fulfillment of magical needs and the receiving of magical supplies), it can be quickly and completely dissolved by any sustained experience of frustrated promise, disappointment, pain. Analysands must learn to "love" the analyst without this kind of primitivity; and then separate from him or her.[10] Pa-

10. It is implicit that there must be a corresponding mastery of the analyst's narcissism in relation to the patient. The challenge involved does vary with each

tients have to learn to tolerate the intense, potentially murderous hatred that accompanies accepting the limitations and at least partial renunciation of narcissistic delusional demands—and go on to enrich themselves by taking in aspects of the analyst's functioning that can be made into their own.

Paradoxically, it appears to me that the defensive stake in narcissism is its power to distance the stress, the danger, caused by the intensity of murderous, primitive instinctual demands. The analyst ought to be able to renounce or at least inhibit his narcissistic and libidinal claims and to be honest about his or her weaknesses and mortality. Freud believed that psychic health consists in the ability to love and to work. Work can be performed with a great charge of narcissistic delusion intact—although some healthy transformation of the most primitive narcissism must of course have been accomplished. But love is more difficult to achieve, and too much clinging to narcissistic delusion can make it impossible.[11] And the

---

particular patient for the analyst, but it is part of professional flexibility to know one's own unconscious and vulnerabilities well enough to be able to operate sufficiently free of narcissism and neurotic tendencies to recognize transferences and countertransferences. When the time for termination of analysis approaches, the analyst must be able to let go of the patient fairly easily as part of a professional obligation toward the patient's welfare—despite inevitable wishes to hold on forever—as the patient struggles to learn how to let go of the analyst. Another way of putting this is to say that the analyst's narcissistic delusions should be well monitored and controlled ("owned"). (This can of course take place fairly freely in the course of attending to emotional reactions to the patient—a regular part of the analyst's functioning—without any conscious awareness of the concept of narcissistic delusions.) The analyst must also avoid taking on as patients people who too strongly evoke his or her regressive and narcissistic tendencies.

11. Walter Scott, *Lay of the Last Minstrel:*

The wretch, concentrated all in self,
Living, shall forfeit fair renown,
And, doubly dying, shall go down

drive to murder, turned against the self or the other, must be dampened. Narcissistic regression is the main defensive way this is brought about. So, paradoxically, we need the very narcissistic regression that can do us in.

I have been suggesting that the primarily (but not exclusively) unconscious representations of the primitive mind—those narcissistic dynamic (and conflictual) vestiges of earliest mental awakenings that both persist in their influence and gain renewed life with regression—when they appear in consciousness, do so in large part as hallucinations and delusions, surrounded, as in dreams, by primary process mechanisms. These ordinary infantile manifestations constitute a kind of normal developmental narcissistic psychotic core that is pervaded by the primary defensive modes of idealization and devaluation: subjectively, bliss and torment; in projection, paradise and hell. With increasing maturation, hallucinations—except for dreams—tend to disappear, but delusions or quasi-delusions, which can be much more unobtrusive and remain hidden both to the self and to others, continue. These emotion-laden early modes of mental operation are full of urgent intensities. They take the form in later life of exigent promises of pleasure and threats of pain, loss, and extinction. We maintain the negative aspects partly in the form of the developmental series of danger situations outlined by Freud. These are never fully worked through, and they often continue on as powerful and DELUSIONAL EXPECTATIONS—expectation of unbearable deprivation, mutilation, loss, extinction. The positive narcissistic delusions (of eternal life, eternal bliss [nirvana], godlike powers) can be viewed as the promise of the self merged with the primary parent forming an eternal, static, sated universe; the concomitant destructive, narcissistic delusional expectations make for

---

To the vile dust from whence he sprung,

Unwept, unhonour'd and unsung. (1805, 74)

torment, rage, hell, and annihilation of self and the universe.[12] These contradictory narcissistic delusional trends are part of what Freud called (in *Totem and Taboo* in 1913) "this narcissistic organization which [I suspect] is never wholly abandoned" (1913, 89). They form a delusional psychotic core based on our earliest (primitive, magical) psychic efforts to deal with our instinctual drives. Freud says,

> I think the meaning of the evolution of civilization is no longer obscure to us. It must present the struggle between Eros and Death, between the instinct of life and the instinct of destruction, as it works itself out in the human species. This struggle is what all life essentially consists of, and the evolution of civilization may therefore be simply described as the struggle for life of the human species. And it is this battle of the giants that our nurse-maids try to appease with their lullaby about Heaven. (1930, 122)

But it is not only the religious who are afflicted with narcissistic delusions. They are a universal and perhaps a necessary burden.

---

12. Destructiveness (murder and suicide) are part of the myth of Narcissus, rooted in the earliest parent/child "mirroring" confrontation and fixation. These primal feelings imbued with death are returned to regressively as a response to later traumata. Meissner (1993) says of the myth, "The classic character whose pathology involved the mirror image and ended in suicide was Narcissus. The water in which he sees his reflection and in which he meets his death [*sic*] is a symbol of birth and the mother. The surface serves as a mirror, but its depth becomes the medium of symbiotic entrapment and death. The myth reflects the earliest mirroring experiences between mother and child that give rise to the rudiments of identity. When such mirroring is optimal, it implies acceptance of the child's separate identity; but where such acceptance and love do not obtain . . . the child's individuation is severely compromised and the resort to pathological and narcissistically determined forms of introjection becomes inevitable" (102).

And healers of the psyche must be able to empathize with this in order to help their patients to be able in turn to empathize with themselves and to become responsible for, to *own,* this burden of delusion.

3

. . . .

MALIGNANT

ENVY

Envy and wrath shorten the life.
—Ecclesiasticus or the Wisdom of
Jesus Son of Sirach

The wise author of Ecclesiasticus couples envy and rage; he implies that envy can be malignant and have a murderous intensity. Freud sees envy as part of our nature and connects it with murder:

When civilization laid down the commandment that a man shall not kill the neighbour whom he hates or who is in his way or whose property he covets, this was clearly done in the interest of man's communal existence, which would not otherwise be practicable. For the murderer would draw down on himself the vengeance of the murdered man's kinsmen and the secret *envy* of others, who within themselves feel as much inclined as he does for such acts of violence. (1927, 40; my italics)

Freud had noted earlier (1909, 226–27) that the Rat Man's envy led him to expect the death of the person he envied.

Melanie Klein, in her monograph *Envy and Gratitude* (1946), writes, "I consider that envy is an oral-sadistic and anal-sadistic expression of destructive impulses, operative from the beginning of life, and that it has a constitutional basis" (ix). She attributes her opinion here to Karl Abraham's work on the destructive impulses and to Freud's hypothesis of the life and death instincts. Abraham had discussed envy as beginning

in the narcissistic period of [the child's] development [when] the child carefully watches over its possessions and regards those of others with jealousy. If anyone has an advantage over it two reactions occur which are closely associated with each other: a hostile feeling against the other person associated with the impulse to deprive him of what he possesses. The union of these two reactions constitutes *envy,* which represents a typical expression of the sadistic-anal developmental phase of the libido. (1920, 340)

A year later Abraham modified his statement, pushing the roots of envy further back into infancy, into the oral libidinal period, and connecting them with cannibalism and greed:

But we will only make a passing reference to the sadistic and anal roots of envy, since both are of minor and auxiliary significance in the production of that character trait, which originates in the earlier, oral phase of libido development. (1921, 382–83)

Envy is one of the seven deadly sins, connected with the work of Satan and of his creatures, like the ancient serpent in the Garden of Eden with which he has been identified. They cannot abide the favored position of the two new innocents in the esteem of the Maker and therefore desire their fall. The envious creatures force their own evil upon Adam and Eve by external seduction. They psychically project their destructive nature onto the first man and woman who identify with it and thus become in part like the evil ones and are cast out of Paradise (as Lucifer, the head of the fallen angels, with whom Satan[1] has been equated, was cast out of Heaven). Envy leads to the first murder; it is what Cain feels toward his younger brother Abel, whom he regards as his father's and the Lord's favorite.

1. Satan (the word is the English translation of the Hebrew word for enemy or adversary; in the Book of Job he is The Adversary) is not present in Genesis; he comes mainly from the Hebrew Talmud and has of course been made much of in the New Testament and in Christian theology.

Envy is often depicted as a hideous woman—a hag having out-lived or been deprived of her fruitful femininity. She frequently has actual or symbolic (e.g., snakes and rods) phallic attributes like the Theban Sphinx or Medusa and is often accompanied by cannibal-istic creatures (cf. Jacques Callot's "Invidia" (envy), one of his se-ries of prints entitled "The Seven Deadly Sins" ("Les Sept Pêchés Cardinaux"). Envy is viewed as wanting what she no longer has or never had.

I am being loosely descriptive rather than scientific in regarding and using *envy*, following Freud, Abraham, and Klein, to denote the emotional representations of destructive aggression in the ear-liest period of psychic development. This primal emotional mix, whatever it is called, can (still somewhat arbitrarily) be mean-ingfully differentiated in later development. The envy, hatred, and greed of later childhood and adulthood alike have undergone enough development and modification to be qualitatively unlike the more diffuse early affects I am calling primal. (Freud felt that hatred developed before love.) We can conceive of this primal emotion as an intense and compelling blend that leads to can-nibalistic and murderous impulses (biting, swallowing, spitting out, tearing, killing, and, later, castrating) associated with teething and the teeth; later on with the cloaca, anus, and vagina regarded as crushing, biting, annihilating sphincters. Psychoanalysts have called these (in my view) innate forces of death and evil narcissistic destructiveness, greed, primal rage, and envy. They of course also arise experientially in reaction to abuse, pain, and frustration.[2] There is no single right or exact term and no need for one. Consid-ering the writings on psychoanalysis, I believe the best case can be made for using *envy*. I am trying to make the concept of early

2. For a balanced view of the current and long-standing controversy about aggression as a drive, see W. Grossman 1993.

destructive affect (whether regarded as innate and/or as reactive to pain and frustration—see Mitchell 1993) more specific for clinical use when I speak of primal or malignant envy. But of course the concept is more important than the words used for it.

Klein differentiated envy from jealousy. Other writers had done so before her,[3] but she is the psychoanalyst who has paid the most attention to envy and the first to try to sketch out its developmental line (as Anna Freud might have put it). Klein sees envy as antedating jealousy.

Envy, wanting what the other has or is, involves (as Klein points out) two people or at least two entities. It is characterized chiefly by an overwhelming conscious feeling of hatred, although it can be directed against someone who is also loved. Klein views it as being there at birth, first directed against the mother's breast and then against the mother. Jealousy (she reminds us) involves three people, and its presence shows that there has been enough psychic development to have at least three people represented in the mind's inner world. "Jealousy is based on love and aims at the possession of the loved object and the removal of the rival" (Segal 1973, 40). I think it is better described as based on an individually varying mixture of hate and love, in which the love is usually more obvious than in envy. Jealousy, Shakespeare's "green-eye'd monster" (from *Othello*) can also exude hate, akin to the murderous hate of primal envy, toward the "loved" or loved object. (Othello, who kills his

3. Crabbe (1816): "We are jealous of what is our own; we are envious of what is another's. Jealousy fears to lose what it has; envy is pained at seeing another have that which it wants for itself. . . . The envious man sickens at the sight of enjoyment; he is easy only in the misery of others: all endeavors, therefore, to satisfy an envious man are fruitless. Jealousy is a noble or an ignoble passion, according to the object; in the former case it is emulation sharpened by fear; in the latter case it is greediness stimulated by fear; envy is always a base passion, having the worst passions in its train" (479).

beloved Desdemona, shows both envy and jealousy of her—he wants, unconsciously, to be her as well as to have her.) Experientially, jealousy exists in an ambience of ambivalence toward both others in the triangle, but in consciousness one of them is wanted (needed and/or loved) and the other is dispensable and to be eliminated. We bring individually varied and dynamically changing admixtures of envy and jealousy to three-person relationships, but these occur after the earliest psychic development.[4]

I don't think we can be certain about what we are born with, and I feel that some of Klein's ideas about how early psychic contents are present are too definite and leave little room for development from a primitive, chaotic beginning. Klein is a pioneer in viewing envy as the first externalized manifestation of Freud's death instinct, but I would question her concept of envy as present (except of course in potentia) from the very beginning of life. I speculate that some glimmering of psychic awareness and differentiation must be present for envy to exist. And conceiving of envy as present at the beginning of differentiation and identity (that is, developing from the time Freud [1938] has empathically characterized as "I am the breast; the breast is part of me") both keeps it early and goes along with Klein's idea that it is first directed against the breast when that is beginning to be felt (or, better, vaguely sensed) as outside the boundaries of the self.

Clinically we are familiar with envy as directed against an other. Envy also can, perhaps with even more primitive derivation, be directed at the sexual parts or functioning of the other—of either gender: breast envy, penis envy, vagina (or, earlier, cloaca) envy, envy of passivity or activity or femininity or masculinity at their

4. In the development of the psychic registration of others in the early infantile representational world (Sandler and Rosenblatt 1962), as in the early development of Greek drama, the third actor is not there at the beginning.

beginning or more developed stages in the other.[5] The envy of what the other has or is would go along with bisexual myths: wanting everything, especially what one does not have—all the holes and all the fillers of holes, the attributes of both sexes at every developmental libidinal stage, as in Plato's myth of the godlike original human bisexual creatures described by Aristophanes in Plato's *Symposium*.

We know that sibling rivalry—the reaction to the arrival of a newborn displacer (again, think of Cain's experience in relation to Abel) or to an older brother or sister who is already there[6]—con-

5. Most of Freud's comments on envy are about penis envy in the female. That penis envy exists, developmentally there for little boys as well as for little girls, seems to me beyond doubt, but I feel that Freud downplayed the boy's envy toward the father's penis and ignored the male's envy of the female. Here is a typical series of quotations that show Freud's antifeminine prejudices—but indignation over these should not lead to denial of the existence and power of penis envy, for both girls and boys: "One cannot very well doubt the importance of envy for the penis. You may take it as an instance of male injustice if I assert that envy and jealousy play an even greater part in the mental life of women than of men. It is not that I think these characteristics are absent in men or that I think they have no other roots in women than envy for the penis; but I am inclined to attribute their greater amount in women to this latter influence. . . . the fact that women must be regarded as having little sense of justice is no doubt related to the predominance of envy in their mental life; for the demand for justice is a modification of envy and lays down the condition subject to which one can put envy aside. We attribute a larger amount of narcissism to femininity, which also affects women's choice of object, so that to be loved is a stronger need for them than to love. The effect of penis-envy has a share, further, in the physical vanity of women, since they are bound to value their charms more highly as a late compensation of their original sexual inferiority" (1933, 125, 134, 132).

6. Freud says of Napoleon's feeling for his elder brother Joseph, "The elder brother is the natural rival; the younger one feels for him an elemental, unfathomable deep hostility for which in later life the expressions 'death wish' and 'murderous intent' may be found appropriate" (1960, 432).

tains murderous rage that mixes envy and jealousy. Freud wrote of this early on:

> Instances of hostility between adult brothers and sisters force themselves upon everyone's experience and we can often establish the fact that the disunity originated in childhood or has always existed. But it is further true that a great many adults, who are on affectionate terms with their brothers and sisters and are ready to stand by them to-day, passed their childhood in almost unbroken terms of enmity with them. The elder child ill-treats the younger, maligns him and robs him of his toys; while the younger is consumed with impotent rage against the elder, envies and fears him, or meets his oppressor with the first stirrings of a love of liberty and a sense of justice. (1900, 250)[7]

There is also for the adult the commonplace envy of the poor for the rich, the lower classes toward the upper classes:

7. Freud later attributes not only the feeling for justice but for communal feeling and group spirit in large part to reaction formations against envy and specifically envy of siblings, although envy of parents would of course also be involved. He speaks of "the initial envy with which the elder child receives the younger one. The elder child would certainly like to put his successor jealously aside, to keep it away from the parents, and to rob it of all its privileges; but in the face of the fact that this younger child (like all that come later) is loved by the parents as much as he himself is, and in consequence of the impossibility of his maintaining his hostile attitude without damaging himself, he is forced into identifying himself with the other children. So there grows up in the troop of children a communal or group feeling, which is then further developed at school. The first demand made by this reaction-formation is for justice, for equal treatment for all. . . . What appears later in society in the shape of *Gemeingeist, esprit de corps,* 'group spirit', etc. does not belie its derivation from what was originally envy. No one must want to put himself forward, everyone must be the same and have the same. Social justice means that we deny ourselves many things so that others may have to do without them as well, or, what is the same thing, may not be able to ask for them. This demand for equality is the root of social conscience and the sense of duty" (1921, 120).

If we turn to those restrictions that apply only to certain classes of society, we meet with a state of things which is flagrant and which always has been recognized. It is to be expected that the underprivileged classes will *envy* the favoured ones their privileges and will do all they can to free themselves from their own surplus of privation. . . . It goes without saying that a civilization which leaves so large a number of its participants unsatisfied and drives them into revolt neither has nor deserves the prospect of a lasting existence. (Freud 1927, 12; my italics)

There is the more basic envy between the generations, the parents envying the child, the child the parents (the old envying the young, the young the old):

When an adult recalls his childhood it seems to him to have been a happy time, in which one enjoyed the moment and looked to the future without any wishes; it is for this reason that he *envies* children. But if children themselves were able to give us information earlier they would probably tell a different story. It seems that childhood is not the blissful idyll into which we distort it in retrospect, and that, on the contrary, children are goaded on through the years of childhood by the one wish to get big and do what grown-ups do. (Freud 1910, 126; my italics)

So children envy adults as adults envy children. Freud (1900) cites an instance of his own envy toward one of his sons, whom in a dream he sees as having had an accident and wearing false teeth:

Deeper analysis at last enabled me to discover what the concealed impulse was which might have found satisfaction in the dreaded accident to my son: it was the envy which is felt for the young by those who have grown old, but which they believe they have completely stifled. (1900, 560)

A displacement of envy toward parents is the envy of superiors: lords and the Lord: "The king or chief arouses envy on account of his privileges: everyone, perhaps, would like to be a king. (Freud 1913, 315)

After the totem animal had ceased to serve as a substitute for him, the primal father, at once so feared and hated, revered and envied, became the prototype of God himself. (Freud 1933, 68)

Freud writes of the universality of hostile envy toward those we call perverts, thereby condemning them in large part because they act out what we all want, consciously or unconsciously, to do too:

These sexual perversions are subject to a quite special ban. . . . It is as though no one could forget that they are not only something disgusting but also something monstrous and dangerous— as though people felt them as seductive and had at bottom to fight down a secret *envy* of those who were enjoying them. [Freud then quotes Nestroy's "famous Tannhäuser parody":

The Venusberg made him forget
Honour and Duty thus—
Strange how these things don't happen
To people such as us.]

In reality perverts are poor wretches who have to pay extremely dear for their hard-won satisfaction. (Freud 1916–17, 321; my italics)

All these forms of envy start from primal murderous, cannibalistic hate and rage at the other (although gradually there develops some neutralization, making for an ambivalent modification that can become compatible with the need, and eventually some kind of love, for the other). The envious hatred for the other (beginning as the first other that is a lost part of the merged self ["I am the breast;

the breast is part of me"]) certainly can be seen as an externally directed, protoexperiential beginning of aggressive drive (our theory is still speculative here) and feeling (the feeling can perhaps obtain clinical access through memory and transference and be validated). The unmodifiably murderous rage at being past one's narcissistic beginnings and driven from the mythical paradise of the womb begins then to be directed at the first other and subsequently—still early on—at all others.[8]

This "there must be no others"[9]—it could be a motto for Narcis-

---

8. It is essential to narcissism that one wants everything—but especially what one does not have and cannot have (what one has is usually depreciated)—so that so much intensity of want and inability to satisfy it result in intense frustration and rage that is part of envy. Similarly, the narcissist wants to be not where he is but where he is not. This is beautifully expressed in Schubert's (1816) "Der Wanderer." The poet (Georg Philipp Schmidt von Luebeck) has the Wanderer say,

> The sun *here* seems so cold,
> The blossoms wilted, the life old,
> And what men say, hollow sound,
> I am a stranger everywhere.
> Where are you, my beloved country?
> Sought for, sensed, but never known!
> The land, the land so green with hope,
> The country where my roses bloom.
> [. . .]
> I wander silently, with little joy,
> My sighs always ask: where?
> A ghostly breath answers back:
> "*There, where you are not, there is happiness!*"
> (my translation; my italics)

The Wanderer, who I see as unhappy, narcissistic, envious, is seeking the mother's breast, the mother's body—the lost place that the other has, where the other is.

9. This is an alternative translation of Solyony's "There will be no successful rivals," quoted from Chekhov's *The Three Sisters* in note 12 below.

sus—amounts to a developmentally unavoidable traumatic potential (involving wanting to get rid of everyone, which is more than can be borne in consciousness). The wish to be the only one supplies the implicit genetic underpinning of one of my favorite quotations, from Lionel Trilling, who states that the essence of moral life is "making a willing suspension of disbelief in the selfhood of someone else" (1955, 94). What is fundamental in this definition is a suspension of primal narcissism[10] (its promise of bliss disguising its murderous propensities: Narcissus waning away at the mirroring spring). Morality and the capacity to love begin with giving up the insistence on being the only one who exists or whose existence matters. We come to be, to varying and ever-changing extent, increasingly capable of abandoning narcissistic positions transiently, on the road toward love. We initially allow others (and again, at first parts of others) to exist insofar as they fulfill our needs. And allowing them a separate actuality beyond this is to begin to value the separate existence of others. The further they are from satisfying our earliest needs and wishes (which center around the universe of the body and its need-fulfilling family extensions), the harder to acknowledge and the less meaningful is the reality of these others.

After much development, and always subject to frequent regression, love is achieved. It first appears in relation to the parents and the family. Love is the conviction of the dearness of the other. With maturity, we can hold onto it for longer and longer periods, but

10. By "primal narcissism" I mean simply the narcissism of early infancy. It should not be confused with Freud's (1914) theoretical concept of primary narcissism: the initial investment of sexual energy by the infant in the ego or self. (Secondary narcissism is defined by Freud as that energy which invests first the mother and then the rest of the external world; it is subsequently withdrawn and reinvested in the ego or self.) See Spruiell 1975 for a different and more comprehensive description of Freud's use of *narcissism*.

probably never without frequent, sometimes considerable, narcissistic regressions. Sleep is a physiological prototype of such regressions; the dream starts out, according to Bertram Lewin, with the self as the only one with the mother's breast as the dream screen—although our dream contents projected onto that screen also display functioning from later developmental periods that allow for some expression of love. Fundamentally though, self-centeredness reigns, and every character in one's dream is at least in part one's self as well as potentially an other.

Regressive narcissistic rage at the other—the feeling that the other has no right to be—is the essence of envy. The emotional mix I am calling primal (or, viewed clinically, malignant) envy has a terrible intensity and a truly murderous quality. Feelings of such destructive intensity are more than a young child can bear, leading to what Freud (1926) calls traumatic anxiety. *That means that experientially the feeling of such rage itself amounts to the basic danger situation of too-muchness which evokes a terrifying expectation of loss of the sense of identity.* Since it is (speculatively) first directed at the breast that is "part of me" and then at (clinically verifiable) the separate part of the parent and ultimately the separate person of the parent, such rage demands that both the self that separates and the parent from whom one becomes separated be eliminated. So, in addition to traumatic anxiety, there is the danger situation of loss of the parent and of parental care. This inescapable developmental trauma becomes the universal and truly terrible trap of primal psychic development, a trap inherent to our initial absolute dependency on the parenting other: wanting to kill off the one we feel we cannot live without, the one who starts off as part of one's self. ("I want to kill you, but without you I am nothing!") Narcissus tries delusionally to become his own other, but insistence on this deprives him of emotional and physical nurturance and so he dies. To remain Narcissus means to insist that there are no

meaningful others, and this cannot be maintained without delusion. Giving up the delusion results in being threatened with
awareness of death and of the wish to kill off others.

In patients one sees this primitive, regressive, murderous manifestation of envy as quite different from the ordinary envy[11] that
expresses wanting what the other has—his or her accomplishments—or even (more hate-filled and more intense) what the
other is—his or her identity. *The most primitive kind of envy seems
to me to be manifested in the associations of a patient by the feeling of
conviction that what the other has or is has been taken away from the
self.* And this primitive cannibalistic feeling has the quality that I
have termed, not altogether happily, delusional. It has a murderous
intensity—a need to get rid of others[12]—that can be terrifying to

11. "Ordinary envy" of course represents a range of feeling—I am lumping
together what is actually qualitatively and quantitatively different for each of us.

12. In the character Solyony from Chekhov's *The Three Sisters,* one sees this
hate-filled claim to be the only one. He is a killer, and he suffers from an amalgam
of jealousy and primitive malignant envy. Chekhov makes Solyony's cannibalistic
nature clear. When the obnoxious Natasha (the other active soul murderer in the
play—see Orgel 1994) brags about the wonderful specialness of her baby, Bobik,
Solyony responds (with a primal malignancy that perhaps stems from sibling
rivalry, specifically, envy of the infant idealized by the mother):

SOLYONY. If that child were mine, I'd fry him in a pan and eat him (224).

Solyony loves and idealizes Irina:

SOLYONY. I can't live without you. [Follows her.] Oh, it's so wonderful just to
look at you. [With tears.] Oh, my joy! Your glorious, marvelous, bewitching
eyes—the most beautiful eyes in the world . . .
IRINA [coldly]. Vassily Vassilyevich, stop it!

He seems to be able to accept that she will not love him. But there must be no
others:

SOLYONY. I've never spoken to you of my love before . . . it's as if I were living on experience, especially for a child. An otherwise predominantly rational and mature person can, at least transiently, be full of irrational conviction that, for example, the analyst's achievement or gifts (e.g., intellectual powers) have been stolen from, have impoverished or deprived, the patient. ("You have everything! And I have nothing!") This cry, when expressive of "What you have has been taken from me," is truly narcissistic envy in that it is directed unconsciously toward an other (the prototype is the mother of early development) who is regarded or claimed as a barely separable part of the self. It follows that with separation, what the separated other has depletes the self, and contact with an other who is perceived as separate is a narcissistic injury. Only with merger can the loss be undone, and a wish for merger is always present. This wish, sometimes conscious, is accompanied by a fear of merger (which again involves a loss of the sense of identity). These are contradictory feelings of terrible intensity, and to feel both in consciousness appears to be unbearable. The unresolvable conflict is frequently handled by recourse to the regressive delusional insistence on blissful merger through idealization: again Narcissus, deluded by Promise, trapped at the mirror/spring.

Oral physiological mechanisms provide a model for the earliest psychological mechanisms of identification (trying to take in the good) and projection (trying to cast out the bad). A (common enough even in the "normal") regressive return to this kind of primal functioning will give rise to a paranoid-like (delusional) reaction involving the projection of something that belongs to the self (idea, feeling, defensive maneuver—separately or in combina-

---

a different planet . . . [Rubs his forehead.] Forget it! I can't make you love me. But there will be no successful rivals . . . I swear to you by all that's sacred that if there's anyone else, I'll kill him. Oh, how wonderful, how wonderful you are! (228).

tions) onto an other. Projection is always delusional in that a (usually felt as bad) part of the self is no longer acknowledged and felt as self. It is no longer owned.

There is another kind of narcissistic delusion not alluded to directly in the last chapter but allied to the feeling of being the only one who exists or the only one who counts: the delusion of being the favorite of the mother (of both parents, of God). (One imagines this is what Chekhov's Bobik would grow up to feel—see note 12 above.) Experientially this delusional or quasi-delusional claim (most relevant to envy and especially to malignant envy) appears in an individually differing mixture of positive and negative forms, since life experiences of frustration and rejection inevitably violate the delusion. The claim continues—alongside some sort of rage at its violation. This last is transiently recognized: "I was and should be mother's favorite—it was promised—but I am not—I will of course be again." The feelings of having been deprived of what was promised—and by someone else (like the other parent or a sibling)—are largely those of malignant envy. If the narcissistic delusional position about maternal promise is predominantly that of deprivation, the resultant predominant malignant envy can reach paranoid intensity.

There are people who appear to be comparatively free of envy, of either the ordinary or the malignant variety. I do regard envy, primal as well as mature, as a universal emotion; but in every person emotions of anxiety, rage, and depression have individual developments and vicissitudes and an individual dynamic range of intensities. These intensities and the quality of the emotion would, of course, vary with the differing individual achievements of mastery that should accompany psychic development—subject to regressions that would revive earlier balances that can for some include a potential preponderance of primal functioning. The achievement of the ability to love is essential in taming primal envy; it may be that the taming of malignant envy is essential to the achievement of the ability to love. (How can one tell which comes first in any individual?) Love neutralizes primal envy—the achievement of the capacity to relate to others can then lead to integrative mastery. As the other becomes precious, one also wants her or him to have everything, to have what one oneself has and wants to have. Few can attain this reversal of malignant envy completely, and none can retain it for long without some regression.

The possession from the start or subsequent development of great gifts and accomplishments frequently helps to ameliorate envy, but not always. As an old man Goethe said (in 1825, when he was seventy-six years old) of his friend and rival Schiller, "For twenty years the public has been disputing which is the greater, Schiller or I; and it ought to be glad that it has got a couple of fellows about whom it can dispute" (Eckermann 1836, 116). Considering this apparent Olympian tranquility, we should remember the murderous sibling rivalry of this former spoiled favorite of a strong mother, which Freud described in his paper "A Childhood Recollection from [Goethe's] *Dichtung und Wahrheit*" (1917). The quotation suggests that, in the main, old Goethe had conquered his envy—he did not need to be the only one; there could be others. This kind of thing would seem easy to say if one had the gifts and had attained the achievements of a Goethe. But contrast this with a story told of the also superlatively gifted Michelangelo in relation to *his* chief rival, the older Leonardo da Vinci. I will quote an account that Robert Fliess (1956) used to illustrate the existence of aggression relatively unmixed with libido (primitive aggression). He first quotes from Gaddiano's *Life of Leonardo*:

> According to the story, Leonardo da Vinci was passing the Spini bank, hard by the church of Santa Trinità, [where] several notables were . . . assembled, who were discussing a passage in Dante,

and seeing Leonardo, they bade him come and explain it to them. At the same time Michelangelo passed, and on one of the crowd calling to him, Leonardo said, "Michelangelo will be able to tell you what it means." To which the latter, thinking this had been said to entrap him, replied, "Nay, do thou explain it thyself, horsemodeller that thou art—who, unable to cast a statue in bronze, was forced with shame to give up the attempt." So saying, he turned his back on them and departed.

Fliess comments: "The example contains all the distinctive elements of the aggressive outbreak under consideration: the subject (Michelangelo) is singularly qualified to appreciate the superiority of the object (Leonardo) whom he must not only attack, but "destroy." Leonardo's existence as an artist is negated; what is left of him is an artisan, and an unsuccessful one at that" (7). This is malignant envy aimed at destroying identity; it has murderous intensity. The reductive attack doesn't affect the relatively secure Leonardo, who perhaps expected it. (The malignantly envious Iago similarly but successfully assaults Othello. When he has suddenly and convincingly aroused the jealousy and envy of the hitherto trusting Othello, the unhappy and devastated Moor expresses the unbearable break in his sense of identity in his *cri de coeur:* "Othello's occupation's gone!" (III/iii/357).)

One sees the direct opposite of malignant envy (as a manifestation of malignant narcissism) in the wonderful book that Rilke (1952) wrote about Cézanne. It has the form of a series of letters from Paris and Prague that Rilke sent to his wife, Clara, over a period of five months in 1907 during which he spent much of his time visiting and revisiting exhibitions of Cézanne's paintings. This was shortly after the painter's death. Rilke declared that Cézanne was one of the chief influences on his poetry. One sees in these letters the moving spectacle of Rilke staring at Cézanne's paintings, interpreting and absorbing the painter's method, defining the essence of Cézanne's art and Cézanne's relationship to his art. Rilke creates Rilke's Cézanne in a manner that profoundly increases the reader's understanding of the painter. Cézanne's paintings and the artist's relation to them are recreated for the reader by Rilke's words in a manner analogous to Cézanne himself staring at a tabletop covered with apples and in his art transforming and recreating them as Cézanne's apples—a transfigured and edifying new reality expressing something essential, "like the kernel in the flesh of the fruit" (Rilke). The poet's absorption in the work and life of the painter makes the poet grow; Rilke's healthy narcissism burgeons through an empathic identificatory relationship to another. Cézanne, as Rilke's Cézanne (in some ways a created character based on a real person in a work of art), becomes a part of Rilke, his ego ideal (see Shengold 1993a). But there is no depletion for the other, for Cézanne, in this swallowing up. It is sublimated cannibalism: eating as loving[13]—a consumption without destruction. What is taken in, identified with, by Rilke is then projected outward to enlarge in turn the image of the other. (Cézanne is created as an other who has acquired a separate existence, although still bearing resemblances to the real object as well as to the creator; he can be loved both as separate from and as part of the creator.) Whatever envy exists toward Cézanne, whatever narcissistic claims are made on him by Rilke, the result is an enhancement of both men and their work in the mind of the poet and in the reader's awareness of the poet's words and the viewer's awareness of the painter's art. We grow by taking on attributes of the other and suppressing rivalry so that both self and other can coexist. One senses in the process of Rilke's making Cézanne an ego ideal a

---

13. Samuel Butler: "I have often said that there is no true love short of eating and consequent assimilation" (1874–1902b, 258).

healthy and creative narcissism transformed into a partial identification which still permits a relationship with the other, resulting in enhanced self-esteem and self-definition on Rilke's part—as a child creatively identifies with a parent. Cézanne is left intact, if anything his significance enlarged in the mind of the reader and not reductively defined, by Rilke's loving, interpretive descriptions. Instead of envy, one sees admiration (I think admiration is part of what Melanie Klein writes of as the capacity for feeling gratitude) as a derivative of love.[14] Love is the enemy of narcissism and of envy.

14. I am grateful to Shelley Orgel for pointing out to me that admiration and gratitude seem inadequate expressions for the positive opposite of *malignant* envy —for its primal opposite; there may not be an appropriate word for this concept. I would think the term would have to refer to some of the promise of bliss that adheres to idealization—developmentally an early defensive mode. There is certainly a range of the antienvy component of the positive feeling for another (paralleling the course of development of the ability to love an other) starting with narcissistically predominant idealization and running through object-related admiration and the more developmentally advanced (and more demanding) capacity for gratitude and beyond—but perhaps the beyond would, with the fullest experience of love, paradoxically hark back toward the blissful intensity of the beginning.

One wonders about the experience of early bliss. One envisions the infant as alternating between potential states of bliss and pain (paradise and hell) that come into their fullness with full satisfaction and acute frustration experienced chiefly in relation to the breast and the mother. But we don't have experiential memories of this (it is the time of the unrememberable (see Frank 1969), and the conditions of life make the overwhelming pain more experienceable than the overwhelming bliss in later life. It is therefore especially difficult to get the right term for what is so hard to conceive of—the proto-object-related states of this time. We are surely dealing with the mysteries of inborn emotional givens and powers ("gifts"), positive qualities about which analysts who specialize in pathology know so little—we specialize in what is wrong. There are infants who seem from the beginning to be predominantly happy and those that seem to be predominantly miserable; and although this can sometimes be for environmentally imposed or physiological reasons, there does appear to be individually different, built-in "wiring." There are

Shortly after I had published my first book, a patient, X, found herself increasingly unable to work on her Ph.D. dissertation. She had been writing a series of papers which would form a book and found that she was unable to finish any of them. There was increasing anxiety and paralysis, and X was under great pressure from her professor-sponsors to get on with her project. X said to me, "If I write a paper, you won't be able to stand it—it will kill you." This was a rather typical projection of part of the patient's envy onto me (and, I repeat, what is projected is not owned—it has delusional quality). That she wanted to kill me as part of her envy was rejected from her consciousness, reversed, and put onto me. About her expressed "conviction that this is true," she said, "The murderous feeling leaves no room for even the possibility of coexistence. You will want me to die. I feel it! I know that this feeling is illogical, but it is only my mind that says that." Several months later X reported that she was about to leave for an unscheduled vacation in order to be with her mother, from whom she had repeatedly declared herself to have separated emotionally. This action followed her doing well in the analysis and in her life. X expressed awareness of need-

---

likewise very young children who as toddlers (and even before) seem actively benevolent (as far as this can be discerned through the veil of their solipsism)—we need not resort to masochism or reaction formation as explanations for their behavior; they appear to be sunny beings able spontaneously to give and share with other children what appears to be predominant enthusiasm and pleasure. We can never know for sure but in our necessarily inexact science I do not see why it cannot be assumed that inborn emotional dispositions account for much—especially in the way of the mysterious abilities that some children show (sometimes even very emotionally deprived and traumatized ones) to extract everything positive from the environment, to survive, to love, and to be playful, humorous, and creative. This involves the mystery of healthy narcissism, which is not an oxymoron. In the later child and adult it can be seen as a higher form of selfishness that includes the ability to love others, alongside some residual quasi-delusional qualities. Healthy narcissism seems very difficult to define.

ing to run away from her gains; but it was not clear whether she was really feeling what she was saying. X was much more certain about feeling anxiety over her anticipation that I would be enraged at not having been told about her plans, which she had made weeks before. She had arranged for the trip after finally having been able to finish one of the chapters of her dissertation. This too she had postponed telling me about: "I have become panicky. I really expect you will throw me out now. I can't think about this. I could say I know better than to expect you to be angry with me but I am absolutely convinced that you are. I am acting and it is stopping my thinking. I am scared." This was followed by a long silence. I felt that the patient was struggling with her anxiety and rage, trying her best not to feel it. This was confirmed by a cry from the heart, "I hate you!" Then there was silence again. This time, when she resumed communicating, it was to express narcissistic regression: "I suddenly have a strange feeling in my whole body. It is as if part of me has become very small here on the couch. I have this heightened sensation of my tiny hand on my enormous chest. And I almost feel as if you are not in this room."

I speculatively concluded that in order to protect me from her murderous envy, she had transiently become both child and parent/breast. This was a regressive defense for her feeling about to be depleted by me in retaliation (having projected onto me her own murderous reaction to the separation and robbing me of my substance by having dared to finish her own chapter). In her regression X had become "I am the breast; the breast is part of me." This was her reaction during the session to dealing with me as the primal parent from whom she was trying to separate, but whom she was terrified of losing.

At the same time, my previously standing for the parent who supported her separation and individuation (expressed by her allowing herself to complete her paper and advance toward maturation) had evoked a primitive terror of losing her mother. This led to hatred of me. X was going back to the original primal parent, her mother, in order to merge with her again. There was murderous destructive envy in transference toward me. (Since I too could be felt as indispensable, this terrible envy was also hard to bear.) These murderous feelings had originally been aimed at her mother's separate big breast, at the big belly her mother had developed before the sibling rival was born, and at that rival (my book was a sibling equivalent). At this point in the analysis, X was not able to bear feeling this rage and connecting it with the past (mother) *and* the present (analyst). But she could not help feeling it for at least short, terrifying periods, especially when idealization and sometimes delusional denial failed, *either* toward me or toward her parents. X first projected her hatred (partly in the form of delusion-filled malignant envy) onto me, and then set out, at first secretly, to return to an idealized mother. This sequence was repeated in the session through feelings and symptoms. (There are obvious competitive negative oedipal dynamics from later development coexistent in this material that I am not dealing with at this time.)

Malignant envy is most likely a potential for everyone, but I have had patients in whom it did not seem to be consciously present. Although everyone feels some sort of "ordinary" envy, most people are rarely aware of feeling the kind of envious hatred that, with its murderous, cannibalistic intensity and the delusional certainty that hedges it, dissolves away all kindly and loving feeling (which might at other times be there in sufficient quantity to neutralize the terrible feelings). But malign envy lurks in the unconscious.

CODA

I want to describe a patient I saw many years ago and was able to follow up on in order to give some perspective on what analysis can and cannot change. I also want to illustrate the developmental processes that can be unleashed by psychoanalysis, processes that can continue after treatment has ended—including continuing self-inquiry (probably the result of identification with the analyst's analyzing functions as well as his or her benevolent and humane qualities, which are not hard to manifest in the privileged position of analyst).

A very successful man, H, a leader in his field, was always complaining that things were too much for him. He had the delusional conviction that almost everyone else, and certainly his analyst, was much better off than he was. Although he performed well at his work and headed his firm, he was subject to a board of directors, and this minimally dependent relationship was a torment to him. He feared rivalry and expected to be replaced by someone the board would prefer to him. He was aware that this reflected a terrible rivalry with his younger brother, who, he could feel, had robbed him of his mother's love. He was aware that his brother was convinced that H had always been the favorite of both parents. Clearly they couldn't both be right, said H, and perhaps he *was* favored—but he had no choice but to feel it the way it came through. As H talked about his childhood, it was apparent that there was not enough love and caring in the home for anyone. The parents were constantly quarreling; the father kept away as much as he could, returning home from his office late at night seemingly only to quarrel, eat, and go to sleep. The mother had been depressed and "crazy"—impulsive, unpredictable, and illogical. She was like a willful and quarrelsome child most of the time, convinced that she was always right. Occasionally she would collapse and could not function. She had alternately smothered H with affection and overstimulation, become furious, and, worst of all, treated him with what seemed like complete indifference.

At work, H characteristically did too much. He couldn't say no to any offer that contained an element of promise, whether this was a gift or some obligation that involved work and payment; he was therefore constantly overcommitting himself. He would then become furious, have a temper tantrum, modeled on his mother's, and often had to get one of his subordinates to fulfill his obligations. H (like Ibsen's Master Builder) would hate this substitute, fearing irrationally that he or she would somehow achieve success and then would eventually displace him as leader. Every bit of publicity, every speech that had to be made, every honor that was proffered had to be H's. He was talented and successful enough to be able to get away with all this, but he was generally disliked, and, in order to be the "only one," he had surrounded himself with weak, masochistic people who sometimes jeopardized the good functioning of his business.

H was constantly furious with me because he felt that whereas he often hated or was bored with his work, I enjoyed what I did and obviously had no difficulty doing it; I was fabulously successful; my parents must have been very rich and bought me a place in medical school. When I, then a very young and inexperienced analyst, asked H how he knew these things, he responded,

> I just know them. They are so and you can't tell me different. There are things I am just sure of.
> I. And you're being sure makes them so?
> H. Yes!

And he meant it. He had taken on the absolute assurance that his crazy mother had so frequently tormented and puzzled him with—a narcissistic regression in her that had often distanced her intermittent frightened uncertainty and depressive doubting. This predominant certainty had a momentum that made her for the most part the dominant leader of the family, steamrollering over any opposition and specifically crushing her husband. He had been consistently degraded and humiliated by her, had reacted with withdrawal, and she had passionately turned to H as a controllable and compliant substitute. H had also been crushed by his mother—and yet (he found this most confusing), apart from jealousy of his brother, he had usually regarded himself as the most important person in the family because she generally had treated him with so much more indulgence than she gave the others. He also became increasingly like his mother and identified with both her domineering and her self-doubting qualities. He hated all rivals and suppressed the hatred of his mother evoked by her overstimulation which frustrated him so; by her forcing him to comply with her whims; and by his feeling that he had to take on her distorted view of the world. As he matured and tried to rebel against her, the terrible vulnerability that her rigid, dominating behavior could not always conceal made his murderous hatred of her increasingly untenable. She developed a chronic illness, which made her even more vulnerable but no less willful and difficult. H largely suppressed all feeling and became what he later called "a competing machine." He had no empathy for his rivals—primarily the father and siblings who had taken his mother away from him. H could not love; and the "machine" defense broke down whenever he was filled with the malignant envy I have described. Good-looking and very talented and intelligent, he was able to cover over much by an ability to be charming and to act *as if* he cared about others, but this was never enough to sustain any kind of loving relationship. He could succeed but he couldn't care.

In the course of years of treatment, much of this emotional deadness was modified, and some of the hate-filled affects could register and be acknowledged as his own. In retrospect, he was astonished that when he started analysis, he had declared his obviously miserable childhood to have been happy. Some work was accomplished in relation to the transference of his feelings onto me; the past was reconstituted in a more meaningful way. When, after some years of analysis, he left to take a job in another city, I felt that he was just starting to come alive as a human being who could relate emotionally. He had become able to experience more of his anxious and depressive feelings and even some joy. He had some old acquaintances toward whom he began to feel closer. He still was not able to care about women except insofar as they fulfilled his sexual and dependent needs. The malignant quality of his envy, especially toward subordinates and beginners, seemed little changed. He did marry. I wondered if he could sustain his marriage and felt he probably would not be able to tolerate having his own children as rivals. This was of course not communicated to him.

H returned to New York City and to treatment many years later, and I discovered that I had been wrong. Not completely wrong: in many ways he had aged but not changed. But there had been a general amelioration of the terrible compulsions that had previously reduced so much of his emotional life. The envy could still, regressively, assume its old terrible intensity. He was much more depressed than he had been. But, almost miraculously, he had continued to emerge as a sentient human being who could care about other people, although he had to struggle to do it. Ambivalence reigned, but he definitely was able to love his wife and especially his children. He had moments of impossible behavior when his raging mother seemed to reemerge in him, but he had become a predominantly good father.

I will illustrate this by interpolating a previously published short paper (Shengold 1993b) about H. It originally had a different purpose from this chapter. I think it shows how H's envy had become less murderous and modified by love for his son and also how envy had been overtaken in large part by jealousy—still a "green-eyed monster" but making for a less destructive mixture of feeling than what H had experienced earlier in his life. He seemed to have attained on his own something of what might have been accomplished if he had remained in analysis: a reduction of the malignant and delusional quality of his envy (which had produced such determined resistance to the analytic process).

H, now a middle-aged man, married, with a seventeen-year-old son taller than himself, had missed a week of treatment to go on a family vacation. He had started an analysis many years before when, as a very young man, he found himself terrified of going on a first European trip. H had realized with surprise that, despite having gone out of town to college and traveled around the country in his early twenties, he was still afraid of being away from his mother for an extended time. He was aware he was irrational but couldn't control the panic. He told me many years later, "I kept thinking that I would get deathly sick and only she could take care of me and save me."

H began the hour I am going to examine by telling about two dreams from the night just before he returned to his sessions after the trip with his family:

Dream 1: My son had some sort of accident. His eyes were blackened and had sustained some sort of damage. I was horrified.

Dream 2: My face was badly cut, as if someone had slashed open my cheek from the mouth to the ear.

Here is the setting of the dreams: H's son John was in the midst of applying both for his driving license and for admission to college. H was proud of his tall, athletic, maturing son and yet distressed that he was going to have to separate from him. He was surprised at how anxious he had become about his son's driving. He had not worried about the boy's involvement in competitive sports even though his own adolescence had been full of his mother's (and sometimes his own) anxieties about the dangers involved in playing football and baseball. Recently John had concentrated more on track and field sports, at which he had become quite adept. H had been painfully aware of his inappropriate anger and envy as his son began to spend more and more time away from home practicing his skills and competing at scholastic track meets. H rationalized that his boy was giving his competitive matches priority over his studies and intellectual interests, but in his analysis he had acknowledged that this was exaggerated. Maybe, H said, he just didn't like his son being away from home so much. And he knew he envied his son's ease with competitiveness, which was so different from his own feeling when he was a teenager or even now.

While on the family vacation, H had given his son some beginning driving instruction. When John told him that he intended to get further lessons from a slightly older friend, H became anxious and immediately felt he ought to intervene and forbid this. His wife had disagreed. H's rage at her made him realize that she was a scapegoat for his anger at both John and John's friend. (Not only envy but jealousy was involved.) Still, he had insisted on driving in the car with the two youths the first time they went out together. H told himself and John that he wanted to make sure how well John's friend drove. He then felt that he had humiliated his son by doing this. Why had he insisted? Only in the session did H realize that John must have been furious with him. And John had retaliated that same evening, H now realized, when he gently discouraged his father from visiting his room for an accustomed presleep talk together. H had felt rejected and hurt.

H told me he did not really distrust John's friend (whose parents H knew and liked) or his driving—and yet H had transiently experienced the young man as if he were a harmful, almost, he realized to his surprise, a sexually threatening presence. This gave H enough grasp of his irrationality so that he was able to suppress his feelings and not interfere further with the driving lessons. (Here the delusional functioning was distanced.) In the hour, H associated to vague memories of homosexual play with his brother "before going to sleep" in the room they shared when he was in latency. These had been brought out in past analytic hours. The experiences had lingered in his mind and in recent years had become connected with worries about his son's masculinity that H felt were not justified by anything in John's behavior. H had several times declared that he must be shifting his fears about himself from the past onto his son.

The frequent nightly periods of closeness between father and son had started at the boy's request when he was nearing puberty. Several years previously, John had said, "Dad, come into my room because when we talk it helps me to go to sleep." The father would lie down at the foot of his son's bed in the dark and they would talk, generally about what each had done during the day. It was a fairly regular, but not an invariable, pattern to do this several times a week. Both father and son had enjoyed these times together. "It's a little like my talking to you when I'm on the couch," H remarked. Much earlier, H was wont to read aloud to his son to help him to get to sleep. (This might be seen as a kind of emotional continuation of the first analysis continued through the years in relation to his son.)

Separation was a conscious and intense psychological danger for H. When he was a child, his father had worked days and evenings, and even when at home had preferred to keep out of his quarrelsome wife's way. The father seemed afraid of his willful, loudly complaining, and demanding spouse, and he didn't interfere when H, her favorite child, was treated as a kind of doll to be kept constantly within mother's reach, as if she were a toddler and H her "security" toy. But this proximity was full of peril for H because his mother was constantly going away: emotionally with her frequent sudden crazy fits of rage, and often physically too—leaving him with his siblings. His mother was a difficult, childish, easily disturbed woman with a whim of iron. She would repeatedly, often without warning, fly into a temper fit ("She could go off like a firecracker"); and afterward would sometimes go back to her parental home to be comforted, staying away for unpredictable lengths of time. H felt alternately so close to her as to be a part of her and so distant that he could just cease to exist for her. When she returned—either by snapping out of her tantrum or, if she had left home, by noisily reentering the house—she would usually again make H the object of her jealous, possessive attention, supervising his every bodily need in a flow of overstimulation. It had taken years of therapy to separate him from his mother sufficiently to get over his need to distance all feelings of tenderness for women and to advance enough from his regressive narcissistic defenses to have any meaningful emotions in a loving direction. He had been able to marry a caring woman and to sustain the relationship. Analysis had helped him to deal with the chronic underlying rage and envy that could so suddenly suffuse him. He had become able to feel it in responsible awareness (that is, to own his anger) and put it in some perspective, but he was not able to tolerate for very long the potential murderous intensity of his feelings, especially of his envy. The automatic temper tantrums in identification with his mother had subsided but occasionally could still occur. He had great difficulty in suppressing this rage when John began wanting to learn to drive the family car. A real rivalry with John had been kindled by the advance in John's maturity and motility.

In the session, H tried to say what came into his mind in association to the details of his dreams. The intensity of his horror at his son's blackened eyes reminded him of what an older acquaintance had once told him of the immense theatrical effect produced on him by Laurence Olivier when the great actor played the scene from *Oedipus Rex* ("the incest play": H) in which Oedipus appears on the stage having blinded himself on discovering the hanged body of his wife/mother Jocasta after her suicide. "I will never forget those black, empty eyes," his friend had said. H concluded from his dream associations that he must have been thinking of his son in Oedipal terms. Was he resenting the boy's growing up? John was taller than his father and had begun to show an interest in girls. (Consciously this had reassured H that his projected homosexual fears were indeed neurotic.) And then in the second dream his own face was cut. Who was Oedipus then—H or his son John? He must read the play—he didn't remember it too well. When I asked, "What about Oedipus's father?" H said he didn't remember anything specific about him.

The next day he came back having read the play and looked up more about Oedipus's father, Laius. Of course he had known that Oedipus had killed his father, but he had not recalled that during his session. He could understand that he was afraid of losing his son but was shocked to realize he would think of him as a rival, especially in sexual terms. (He had neglected the murderous father/son confrontation.) H, like so many others, found it easier to think about the heterosexual incestuous themes than the negative homosexual ones and, perhaps showing even deeper conflict and danger, felt more comfortable in thinking of the sexual than the murderous impulses involved in the Oedipus complex.

Oedipus's father has a particular connection with homosexuality. Laius has been called the first homosexual in history (Zeus came first among the gods in his rape of Ganymede)—see Kouretas 1963. Robert Graves, in his book on Greek myth, expounds:

Laius, when banished from Thebes, was hospitably received by Pelops at Pisa, but fell in love with [Pelops's son] Chrysippus, to whom he taught the charioteer's art;[15] and, as soon as the sen-

15. Laius promoted locomotion in his catamite, Chryssipus, while he inhibited it in his son, Oedipus, whom he crippled. I do not know if H knew anything about this (he didn't tell me what he had read), but Laius did teach Chryssipus to drive.

tence of banishment was annulled, carried the boy off in his chariot ... and brought him to Thebes as his catamite. ... Some say that Laius ... was the first pederast; which is why the Thebans, far from condemning the practice, maintain a regiment called the Sacred Band, composed entirely of boys and their lovers. (1955, 41–42)

Here is Oedipus's account of the murderous encounter with Laius in *Oedipus Rex* (translated by Fitts and Fitzgerald):

> There were three *highways*
> Coming together at a *place I passed*;
> And there a herald *came towards me,* and a *chariot*
> *Drawn by horses,* with a man such as you describe
> Seated in it. The groom *leading the horses*
> *Forced me off the road* at his lord's command:
> But as this *charioteer lurched over towards me*
> I struck him in my rage. The old man saw me
> And brought his double goad down upon my head
> As I *came abreast.*
>
>   He was paid back and more!
> Swinging my club in this right hand *I knocked him*
> *Out of his car, and he rolled on the ground.*
>   I killed him.
>
> I killed them all.
> (Sophocles, 41; I have underlined the images of locomotion)

The parricidal struggle took place on the highway (at the place where three roads meet—symbol of the mother's genitals); driving a vehicle and a struggle over the rights of locomotion are involved in the battle. Laius strikes Oedipus on the head, possibly on the face (as in H's dream).

Laius, king of Thebes, had been on his way to Delphi to ask the oracle how he could get rid of the monstrous Sphinx that was devastating travelers to Thebes. Graves notes that Hera had sent the murderous Sphinx to punish Thebes for Laius's abduction from Pisa of the boy Chrysippus he had fallen in love with (1955, 10)—a linkage of murder and bisexuality, more specifically of murder as a punishment for homosexuality.

After killing Laius, Oedipus had continued toward Thebes, where he defeated the Sphinx by guessing her riddle, causing the monster to kill herself as Jocasta was later to do when she had to face the truth of her relationship with Oedipus. I quote from an article I wrote in 1963, "The Parent as Sphinx":

> Mahler and Gosliner (1955) describe the "symbiotically overanx-ious psychotic mother": "The mother's hitherto doting attitude changes abruptly at the advent of the separation-individuation phase [that is, when the child attains the power of locomotion].
> ... It is the maturational growth of locomotion which exposes the infant to the important experience of deliberate and active body separation from and reunion with the mother" (201, 195).[16] It follows that it is the child's standing up and walking away, out of the symbiotic unit, that these potentially soul-murdering moth-ers cannot tolerate. With this in mind, here is the riddle of the Sphinx: "What being, with only one voice, has sometimes two feet, sometimes three, sometimes four, and is weakest when it has the most?" Oedipus's solution: "Man—because he crawls on all fours as an infant, stands firmly on his two feet as a youth, and leans on his staff in his old age" (Graves 1955, 10).

The entire riddle is about locomotion—the ability to move away from the mother—and in answering it Oedipus establishes

---

16. I equate the psychotic mother from ontogenetic development with the phylogenetic primal bisexual parent (symbolized by the Sphinx). But of course this monstrous imago is there in all of us to varying degree (and therefore is attached to all parents) as part of the heritage of infantile development.

his separate identity and manhood. Instead of suffering the fate of the defeated challenger—being devoured by the monster (thus reestablishing the symbiosis)—the victorious Oedipus watches the Sphinx hurl herself to her death. . . . For this great deed Oedipus was awarded the city and his mother—symbol and thing symbolized—which meant he could now have his mother and need no longer be part of her. With this heroic step the child's developmental transition away from symbiosis becomes possible. Normal identification and object relationship with the separated mother allow the child to move from the preoedipal relationship with the mother to the oedipal. (1989, 44–45)

The distressing dreams about his son had occurred some months after H had suffered the death of his own father, which partly conditioned the sparseness of his associations to the dreams in the sessions I have quoted from. The dreams were dealt with more thoroughly later in the analysis.

It is not only H who can become Oedipus (and Laius and Jocasta) in dreams. Sophocles' Jocasta says this in an effort to minimize Oedipus's fears about the prophecy that he will bed his mother and kill his father:

Have no more fear of sleeping with your mother:
How many men, in dreams, have lain with their mothers!
No reasonable man is troubled by such things. (57)

We are all Oedipus (women as well as men), and we must all destroy the Sphinx—distance ourselves from the earliest inner pictures (self- as well as object representations) based on our earliest primitive imagos of our parents. Paradoxically, these feelings of destructive intensity—derived from primal affect (this would involve malignant envy)—also bind us to our parents. The bisexual Sphinx, symbol of the primal parent, also alludes to the basic destructive and bisexual nature of all human beings—the primitive drives which are again so subject to denial by some modern psychoanalytic theorists. Perhaps the hardest part of the Oedipus complex to bear experientially are those emotions evoked by the figure of the murderous and cannibalistic Sphinx—the primitive rage to kill. Oedipus ends his speech about the fatal meeting with Laius:

I killed him.
I killed them all. (41)

In current psychoanalytic theory (at least for those who do not deny drive theory), the developmental continuation of primitive, preoedipal functioning into later, oedipal functioning (confluence rather than either/or) is a commonplace.

This clinical excerpt demonstrates the essential, inseparable interlinkage of drive and object relations in psychic development: how separation and individuation as expressed in the ability to move away from the parent (locomotion) are implicated in sexual and aggressive conflict. It is also my impression that we need reminding—in our feelings perhaps more than in our theory—that there are preoedipal developmental mixtures of sex and murder that continue to influence us alongside and underneath the later, more bearable (more "fused" and "neutralized," less exigent) oedipal ones, giving rise to feelings both more exigent and unbearable which come to life with regression. (In this book I have emphasized the more inclusive early narcissistic ["preoedipal"] primitive psychic functioning with its delusional quality—of which these feelings are a part—that underlies the later psychic development.) My patient H's dreams and associations brought these conclusions back into my awareness with the vividness of the timeless tragic drama—literary and human—he had evoked.

In relation to his children, H's envy, while still present and troublesome, had been divested of some of its terrible, malignant intensity and much of its delusional quality. By becoming able to love his son and allow for separation from him, H showed the result of the developmental steps he had been able to take—steps away from (= locomotion) the murderous primal parent Sphinx, a symbol of omnipotent, cannibalistic envy who devours and absorbs all others.

I have defined envy and jealousy, following Freud, Abraham, and M. Klein. Envy is depicted as starting in the earliest period of psychic development and having at first the characteristics of primal psychic functioning. As envy (a two-person process) develops along with the maturing psyche it gets modified by loving feeling and is accompanied by jealousy (a three-person process). But malignant envy is a retention of, or a regression to, the infant's original primal murderous intensity ("There must be no others!")—an intensity that gets reacted to defensively by projection and delusion formation. Descriptively and clinically, malignant envy involves feeling specifically that what the envied other has or is has been stolen from the self. It has a delusional quality that makes it a formidable resistance to treatment; this has to be acknowledged by the patient before it can be owned and analyzed toward its attenuation.

4

. . . .

PARANOID

DELUSIONS

AND DELUSIONS

ACQUIRED BY

IDENTIFICATION

WITH DELUSIONAL

PARENTS

We cannot get rid of persecution; if we feel at all we
must persecute something; the mere acts of feeding
and growing are acts of persecution.
—Samuel Butler, *Notebooks*

Samuel Butler, that misanthropic curmudgeon ("The best of
friends must meet" [Butler 1874–1902a, 533])—hater of Father,
the fathers and mothers of this world, and of women—is here
pointing out the universality of feelings of persecution and the
relevance of this phenomenon to the earliest (oral, cannibalistic)
period of life. I will be using Samuel Butler as a literary example of
my clinical ideas in the next chapter.

One important clinical implication of malignant envy is that it
has an inherent paranoid potential. If I feel that you have taken
away from me something of mine or something that should be
mine, then you are persecuting me and I hate you and have the
right to avenge myself and persecute you. This is simply spelling
out some of the rationalization for projection (the casting out of
the self what is bad and hateful onto another); and projection can
result in its deepest and most delusional form in paranoid phenomena: the range (put in order of increasing delusional intensity)
from transient paranoid feelings to paranoid quasi-delusions to
paranoid delusions of everyday life to psychotic paranoid delusions. (The latter would be fixed, intense, and threaten to or actually succeed in massively taking over or at least influencing a large
part—typically not all—of the individual's psychic functioning.)
Most banally, paranoid delusion in its common, everyday, and
usually relatively diluted and transient form appears in the hate-

filled prejudices that everyone possesses—involving for example the deindividualization and even dehumanization of other human beings. The white driver whose car is passed by a speeding black driver feels enraged and thinks, or sometimes says, or even yells, "Fucking nigger!"; the black man in a reversed situation feels enraged and thinks, or sometimes says, or even yells, "Fucking honkie!" Any given individual could be ashamed of the malevolent prejudicial reaction, or embrace it with conviction, or something in between—but we would all be subject to it. Envy of the superior in competition is involved (including in my example what could be called castration envy—the rage, of the child of either sex, at the superior genital). The person from another race, Freud has taught us, can symbolize the parent: the incestuous object and/or the once impossibly superior rival. So, with myriad individual variations, these delusional vestiges of prejudice, which of course can be full of positive feeling as well as of hatred, are universal.

Arnold Cooper, in a paper entitled "Paranoia: A Part of Most Analyses" (1993), observes that under the regressive conditions of psychoanalysis paranoid defenses and other aspects of paranoia appear regularly even in "neurotic patient[s] without borderline features" (437). Cooper sees these phenomena as manifestations of preoedipal conflicts—the inevitable inner turmoil of our earliest years. It would follow that paranoid events (both those predominantly involving discharge and those predominantly involving defense against expression) would be there in everyone—appearing in daily life and not only as by-products of the analytic process. Cooper speaks of "the everyday paranoid" (439). (Cooper provides an excellent description with clinical illustrations as well as pertinent references by psychoanalytic authors to back up his observations.) I too intend to describe the paranoid (delusional, quasi-delusional) phenomena of everyday life in the nonpsychotic.

Melanie Klein, trying to spell out the vicissitudes of the infant's

inherent aggressive drive (following Freud, who connects the clinical manifestations of aggression in his theory with an instinctual
drive he pictures as a derivation of a hypothesized death instinct),
feels that there is a stage of development when the infant assumes
what she calls the "paranoid/schizoid position" during which paranoid functioning is the norm. That functioning is subsequently
subject to fixation and regression that affects subsequent life. Paranoia seems to me to be based on both an early (primal) universal
form of defense: projection; and on what is projected: primal affects—various combinations of murderous, hate-filled, cannibalistic, and early sexual feelings. Projection of (1) malignant envy,
and—as Freud (1911) points out—of (2) forbidden sexual, and
perhaps most often homosexual, feelings of attraction that is then
reversed into feelings of hatred and persecution (envy and sexual
feelings are of course not at all mutually exclusive) results in paranoid moments and in paranoid illness (cf. Blum 1980).[1] The casting out of the bad onto others dehumanizes those others. They—
the enemies—are either monsters and persecutors or victims and
deserving of persecution. They are stripped of their humanity;
both sympathy and empathy are dimmed or banished. This turning others into nonpeople in order to be able to torture and kill
them is seen, as a mass phenomenon, in the atrocities of warfare—
by both sides: enabling the perpetrator's actions and conditioning
the reactions of participants of both sides. Murder is permissible
against Them.

There can be no certainty about the existence of a death instinct.
I do believe in aggression as an inborn phenomenon (an instinc-

1. Blum (1980) stresses the importance of preoedipal psychic development to
paranoia: "All levels of psychosexual development and their corresponding danger
situations contribute to the transformed fantasy of persecution and punishment:
early infantile narcissism, aggression, and sadomasochism are especially important" (359).

tual drive) as well as recognizing it as an observable result of inevitable environmental, and specifically parental, frustration that occurs in the course of development and maturation. The baby is born with some set of biologically derived, inherited emotional dispositions, undoubtedly affected by the intrauterine environment (physiochemical and perhaps psychological/chemical influences from the pregnant mother) and from early experiences after birth. Infants can be born with many kinds of deficiencies and excesses that can make even the most ideal maternal care insufficient. Early traumata and loss, hateful parental rejection, overstimulation, and deprivation by the mothering figure can, separately and in various combinations, give rise to psychopathological manifestations of all sorts. These environmental influences specifically cause the burgeoning of the intense rage that is probably inherited as a large component of primal emotions—murderously charged, somatically pervaded and pervasive. The infant attempts to hold onto the good—that which gives pleasure and relief from pain (and promises bliss)—and to project outward what is felt as painful and bad (and promises catastrophe). As described in the previous chapter, the projection has to go first to a separating part of the "breast/me" and then to the separated psychic representation of the mother's breast and subsequently to the whole mother. There eventually results in the young child's mind (its psychic representational creation, as it were) the presence of the bad primal parent, the cannibalistic bisexual creature (like the Sphinx) who devours its offspring and is split off from the idealized, angelic, good primal parent who comforts and rescues. We are familiar with these opposites in the disguised, projected, and generalized forms of a bad god and a good god, Satan and the Lord. The infant's self-representations, similarly, tend to split into good and bad. Early development is marked by this terribly intense, melodramatic split into extremes: paradise or hell, bliss or torment, good or bad, black or white. (Modulation and integration come only slowly—after much maturation—and incompletely—with constant vulnerability to regression.) The good is taken in, swallowed—the bad is rejected, spit out. The oral physiological mechanisms provide a model for the earliest psychological mechanisms of identification (trying to take in the good) and projection (trying to cast out the bad).

A regressive return to this kind of functioning will give rise to a delusional reaction involving the projection of something psychical, conscious or unconscious, that belongs to the self—idea, feeling, defensive maneuver (separately or in combinations) onto an other. Projection is always delusional[2] in that a (usually "bad") part of the self is no longer acknowledged and felt as self. *It becomes "not-me" and it is no longer owned.* Not all delusions are paranoid delusions, but all paranoid manifestations are at least in part delusional.

What constitutes the bad changes in the course of early psychic development. Freud has outlined a gamut of danger situations that children traverse as psychic structure matures and develops. What is initially overwhelming (the first danger situation is that of over-stimulation and traumatic anxiety) gradually becomes more tolerable as the brain and mind mature. The bad cannot continue to be avoided with impunity; it must be acknowledged and registerable in order for the child to deal with (by way of defense and adaptation) both the bad as part of vicissitudes of the internal drives and the bad as part of the nature of external reality. With maturation

2. Freud talked about the kernel of truth that often exists in the paranoid delusion; that is, what one projects from one's self can actually correspond to something already there in the other. When this happens it can easily be rationalized; not only is the quality projected onto the other disowned, but the delusional nature of the paranoid conviction is further covered by righteous rationalization.

and development the nature of the bad changes; new danger situations and unacceptable feelings, ideas, and situations continue to accrue alongside the old ones. But a general modulation of intensity in psychic dynamics continues past the predominant mastery of primal functioning; and a gradual acquisition of the power to test reality modifies the initial delusional qualities. Of course some early mental tendencies persist (this is what is meant by fixation) and, always, some get revived with frustration and other conditions that bring on regression.

A capable and attractive young woman, F, entered analysis principally because she had experienced a series of sexual relationships either with men who turned out to be unreliable and uncaring or with men toward whom, if they seemed to be of good character and really to value her, she felt unattracted. Also, she reported finding it easy to achieve success that was often followed by an attempt to undermine her own achievements. This was a reluctant insight; she usually initially rationalized her failures and blamed them on someone else, sometimes with a fury that alarmed her.

F's outline of her chief complaints turned out to be a kind of predictive pattern for the beginning of her analysis. Initially F felt very positive about the work and about me; she tried very hard to report her associations; she was able to face up to some very difficult feelings, including some sexual feelings, distrust, and anger toward me. She was a hardworking, seriously motivated, psychologically adept analysand. I found myself looking forward to her sessions. Although F was not in the healing profession, she performed like an experienced colleague. I realized that there was a lot of defensive intellectual distancing as well as talent involved in this superior functioning, and I thought of Freud's description of some patients whose resistances *seemed* to be in abeyance in what he called an initial honeymoon period.

One day there was a sudden increase in emotional and sexual

intensity. It came shortly before my first long vacation during a session in which F was describing her sexual affairs. For the first time she described specific details about sexual events: kinds of contact, body parts, her physical and emotional reactions, and even some of her sadomasochistic fantasies. This detailing seemed to evoke somatic motor expression on the couch. F appeared to be restless and uncomfortable, often shifting her position, crossing and uncrossing her legs. I felt but did not interpret that she was experiencing and was in conflict about the sexual excitement she was describing. At the end of the session, she got up from the couch to leave. For the first time, she paused awhile, standing in profile, then half-turned and stared at me with a glance full of hatred that evoked in me the thought, "If looks could kill I would be dead." F hesitated a few moments and then uncharacteristically strode briskly out of the office, slamming the door.

The next day she started her hour in a fury. This, too, was a first. F had been able to express anger toward me before; most of this had been inappropriate and undeserved—obvious transference phenomena—but on the few occasions when I had done something that properly evoked her anger, F had dealt with the anger fairly calmly and was able to work with it in the analysis. But now the basilisk that had emerged at the end of the previous session seemed to have become further transformed into a kind of harpy, full of accusatory rage. I felt she was showing me something of what she had initially talked about—her rage when she blamed others for her failures at work. The sessions began as a verbal (= oral) attack. I had never before heard her speak in the intense tone of righteous fury she assumed; it was as if an entirely different person had emerged:

I am furious with you because of what happened yesterday. I

know that you were sexually excited. You were looking at my breasts when I got up off the couch. Don't try to deny it! I *know* it was so. I feel so much distrust for you now. I had to struggle with myself to come back here. I don't know if I can continue to work with you. I feel as if I have suddenly discovered what you are. I've been furious ever since I left here. I *know*[3] you are going to deny all this and try to brainwash me. I hate you and I can't stand this feeling!

There followed an unprecedented long period of silence which lasted most of the session. Toward the end of the hour, F, resuming her familiar calm tone of voice, simply recited some of the events of her working day. Seemingly, in the interim, she had banished, isolated away, the harpy persona.

For a few sessions F continued on as if the disrupting rage and accusation, what I took to be a transient paranoid reaction, had never occurred. When she showed some mild anger the following week, I noted the contrast to the intensity of her last angry expressions and wondered aloud why she had subsequently so completely ignored her outburst and her accusations. She became apologetic. "I showed you a side of me that I can't stand. It is *as if* it just happens and then I forget about it as quickly as I can. Last week I felt that terrible anger with you for a whole day. After that second session with the awful silence, I didn't go back to work. I felt so upset and then so sleepy that I just went home and went to bed. I slept for twelve hours and when I woke up it was *as if* it hadn't

3. The emphasis of these "I know's" resembles that of the "she's" (= "they's") of my patient M, whom I mentioned and characterized as paranoid in chapter 1 above.

been" (my italics—not the patient's emphasis). F had, it turned out, also struggled with "sleepiness" during the silence of that session— the resumption of talk during the last minutes of the hour had also had an "as if" quality. The sleepiness turned out to be F's tendency to go into an altered state of consciousness. She was given to what Fliess (1953) calls "hypnotic evasion" (see Shengold 1978, 1989). Here I was just becoming aware of the presence of F's extensive use, in and out of her analytic sessions, of this predominantly but not exclusively defensive maneuver. It became obvious later in the analysis that F would, without the autohypnotic shift, feel intense anxiety as she began to feel furious anger.

F had, up to age eight or nine, slept in a small room adjoining her parents' bedroom. The connection was an archway; there was no closable door. F at first did not remember witnessing any sexual encounters between them. (Later on there were primal scene memories, at first of isolated specific details, some of which appeared to be distorted, and then of fuller sequences that enabled her to feel certain she had repeatedly heard and seen parental intercourse.) At this stage in the analysis, F described the frequent, and for the child terrible, quarreling that went on between the parents. These quarrels had two main subjects: money and in-laws—hatred of one another's family. F remembered repetitive scenes of shouting, screaming, cursing, weeping—often ending in physical fights. F had been terrified that one or the other would be killed: "Father would usually seem to win, but Mother was even fiercer than Father." The child, when she reached school age, was convinced that her parents would get a divorce—a not uncommon fate of the marriages of many of the parents of her friends. This additional expectation of loss was also felt as unbearable. Later in the analysis, it became clear that these fights frequently would, past the real or at least the show of violence, end in sexual intercourse.

There was also a "free" family policy of nakedness, openly championed as the thing to do. This was described more as parading, rather than simply walking around, in the nude. An atmosphere of family righteousness, being entitled to aristocratic privilege for their superior ways, was characteristic of both parents. Each had come from "old money," Protestant, upper-class families who had lost their wealth but not their elite pretensions. Both families were rife with alcoholism, and F's parents too were heavy drinkers. The drinking seemed to facilitate both the quarreling and the exhibitionistic nudity.

Although F's father and mother could stand together against mutual enemies, or people who were declared to be mutual enemies, they frequently appeared to be, in F's view, viciously hostile to one another. The children were often used as go-betweens, especially for financial negotiations when the parents were not speaking to one another. More devastating was the use of the children for purposes of emotional blackmail. F's descriptions made me feel that each parent enacted and was obsessed by an intermittent paranoid (she never used the word) scenario in which the other and his or her family played the role of persecutor. But this atmosphere of recurrent pervasive hatred, so damaging and terrifying for the children, seemed to have functioned as emotional glue for the parents. Quarreling and family paranoia was their way of connecting and staying together. They were both continuing their ways into old age when F was coming to analysis. This provided the possibility of current validation which eventually made F's conviction about the past easier, especially when she began to modify her autohypnotic, as if, and isolating defenses as the analysis progressed.

The parents had postponed having children until they were approaching forty. F was the oldest child. It became her role to be the good one, the one who looked after the welfare of her younger sibling (servants never stayed very long) and, even, of the parents. (She remembered pulling the covers over their naked bodies on mornings when they were sleeping late after drunken parties.) F's maternal role in the family was, she felt, appreciated. But on the infrequent occasions when mother or father became furious with her, F was devastated. More often she felt ignored (especially when they had been drinking) or taken for granted by them. The misery and anger that this not being cared about caused was largely suppressed. Beneath her role as the good girl was intense and even murderous rage. Some of this burst into action in adolescence—in secret rebellion that almost amounted to sexual promiscuity and in experiments with taking drugs. In college she had started longer sexual relationships with men, but—as she had initially described —these never worked out to be loving or even satisfactory.

The primal scene traumata seemed to me to be connected with the murderous stare produced by her conviction that I had become sexually excited and voyeuristic (both F's projection and transference) during the hour I first described. What was more subtly concealed and much harder to modify was F's identification with the raging, sadistic, paranoid aspects of both parents. This identification (she could become, rather than see and react with rage against, the parent) was an unconscious way of saving them from being killed off by her murderous rage, since it was then directed against dispensable others; this had begun with her siblings but was also directed against herself. There was the constant danger of the rage turning toward the original indispensable objects or, as with me, their much-needed substitutes. Any real emotional closeness and dependency, so longed for consciously, were avoided.

The transient paranoid delusions were rare, hedged in and isolated by her obsessional and autohypnotic defenses. They were repeated, but they were not owned. They formed a largely unacknowledged part of herself that she treated almost as if it were a separate personality. To use her term, she "pretended away" from the murderous, accusatory, sadomasochistically exciting, terrifying, righteous externalization of this inner representation of her parents which had become a hidden part of her self. The delusional qualities, appearing intermittently, were there by way of identification with those aspects of her parents that had made her feel hostile toward and deprived and persecuted by them. She protected her split-off inner picture of the much-needed good parent by becoming the split-off bad parent and turning the murderous rage onto others and onto herself. This rage was felt only in attenuation and rarely enacted or even allowed into consciousness for long.

I do not believe paranoid delusions of the everyday variety need always come from identification with parents. There are patients with transient paranoid delusions whose parents do not demonstrate the paranoid qualities that the parents of F definitely possessed in a minor way—they were certainly neither paranoid characters nor paranoid psychotics. (Their paranoid qualities affected F less than their characteristic indifference: lack of empathy and not caring enough.) Of course the ubiquity of paranoid mechanisms (as I see it) can always make identification a possible source, but it is not necessarily a strong one.

I think it is apparent by now that the categories created by my chapter headings are arbitrary and that most patients with the delusions of everyday life I am describing are suffering from combinations of all of them. Narcissism, envy, paranoid mechanisms often occur together and, indeed, are most often blended together. Often, but not always—at least not always in ways that can be documented and appear to be significant—these delusions and quasi-delusions are also involved with experiences and identifications with delusional parents that begin in childhood. The case of F showed paranoid tendencies which seemed in large part to be the product of identification with her parents.

A male patient, J, torn by contradictory wishes of many kinds: wanting to be active and masculine and "good"/wanting to be passive and feminine and "bad"; wanting to be sadistic/wanting to be masochistic (both "bad) and neither ("good"); wanting to be dirty ("bad")/wanting to be clean ("good"); wanting to be a baby ("bad")/wanting to be an adult ("good"). J consistently tried to juggle these impossible combinations, to preserve all options as it were, by intermittent narcissistic regression. In the analysis he was beginning to become aware of this. But the prospect of losing any part of his wishes terrified him, and he was used to denying the ultimately destructive and masochistic price that he had to pay to preserve the stagnation necessary to maintaining the juggling. He was able to get around what sometimes amounted to paralysis in his career and in his relationships by acting as if he were his best self: "good," masculine, active, clean, adult. And he was gifted enough to be able to make adaptive narcissistic use of his intelligence and charm to simulate his way toward a series of successes which he promptly would begin to compromise as soon as they were achieved. The recognition of this pattern terrified him; he knew that it was true, but he felt obliged to deny it. He used the delusional promise of bliss to keep away from the delusional terror of catastrophe that was there for him in relation to losses of any kind. Basically he appeared to me to dread the giving up of the wishes to be indulged by, sexually connect with, and ultimately to merge with and become his very grandiose, overindulgent, seductive mother—a paranoid woman of aggressive righteousness (terrifying everyone in the family with her wrath), insistent on having her way, but fundamentally dishonest and unreliable. Any attempt to resist her whim meant the danger of being cast out with the rest of the hostile and despised world not reigned over by this narcissistic queen—F would become one of Them—the enemies. F was able to describe and even to complain bitterly about and condemn his mother's failings; but he would then reverse himself and deny what he had declared. This would be followed by his assuming the "bad" aspects of his mother's character himself, turning on and making use of others seductively, aggressively, dishonestly. He would have transient periods of narcissistic and paranoid behavior.

Another patient, V, did not seem able to grasp the analyst's announcement of a forthcoming vacation. She kept bringing it up, getting the dates wrong, and seemed to be trying to provoke correction and scolding. I interpreted her fear: I said that perhaps she was too afraid of the separation to be able to register clearly what was going on; and that perhaps she was again trying to hold on to me by provoking a quarrel. (This was a long-established pattern and was not the first time I had pointed it out. Her mother had often done this, provoking a controversy every morning when her husband went out to work and the children went out to school.) V responded in a way that made me feel that she was giving more than the perfunctory, "Yes, yes!" that had been the rejoinder on previous occasions:

> I *am* terrified of separation and of what will happen when you go away. And it is true that I can't think about it. My mind gets fuzzy. I do expect that you will be critical and cruel. I feel sure you won't tell me when you are going away now that I've provoked you, *and suddenly*[4] you will be gone.

V went on to tell me that her husband, for her birthday, had given her a necklace the design and color of which "perfectly" matched a recently purchased favorite dress. His thoughtful care had made her so happy. But when she showed the gift to her mother, her mother said, with venom in her voice, "Those beads are square; beads should be round." "And then all the joy drained out of me," V added.

---

4. I have commented on the "and suddenly" phenomenon in the first chapter as often relating to the traumatized child's expectation of a sudden, terrible transformation in the parental figure. Here it figures, as it does frequently, as a delusional expectation.

I feel that this story has many connected layers of meaning. This mother was always complaining about everyone in the family and never had a good word to say for anyone except herself. The mother was both jealous (this was easiest for the patient to deal with) and envious and therefore hostile to V and to her husband. She wanted to be the recipient of all the gifts, and in that sense to be the patient with a loving husband; on the deeper level of envy she wanted to be the patient's husband and have the patient to herself.

It was characteristic for this mother, as she was portrayed by the patient's words (and dramatized in the patient's intermittent identificatory enactments), to be unable to empathize with or care about an individual seen as separate from herself. Either the child fulfils the mother's need or the child doesn't count. It was predictable that the mother would not care that her daughter was made happy by her son-in-law's considerate fondness. This mother had turned to her five-year-old daughter as a combination of plaything and companion when she had been deserted by (or more probably had driven away) her husband. The child had been used as an extension of herself, as a fleshed-out accompanying shadow (unless someone better turned up, but that never lasted for long), and, more damaging, as an auxiliary to the mother's masturbation.

Any feeling of the mother's deficiencies and depredations or any awareness of the reflection of these in herself led V to a terrifying intensity of rage. It was difficult and sometimes impossible to sustain this for long, even enough to use as a signal. The "sheer murder" between mother and child (and V played both roles) led to panic—led to the basic terror of overstimulation ("too-muchness") and also to the fear of irreversible loss initiated by separation. The panic would initiate a number of defensive operations which featured reversal and denial of the rage: idealization of the mother; reducing all feelings to nothing; giving into her mother and mollifying the mother's anger by taking on guilt and a feeling of bodily and specifically genital unworthiness; most frequently by identifying with the mother.

When she emerged, by way of repetitive identification with her mother—V's predominant way of preserving her paranoid mother from the daughter's murderous impulses—V would enact the mother's sadism and feel and express the mother's righteousness: "Mother would never admit that she was wrong in any way." Transiently and repetitively, V herself would become vicious and paranoid, as "crazy," as driven and protected by delusions as her mother. Responsible awareness of this was minimal. In her current life, denial of what she herself did and said every day to her family in her assumption of her mother's sadistic persona came only afterward, when she could be "sorry."[5] But this did not in any way prevent the repetition of the tormenting words and actions the next day. Registration of the past had been interfered with by the childhood traumata; V could not own the imago of the tormenting mother who lived on in her mind long after the mother's death— and who emerged periodically, like an unexorcized demon, to take over V's identity. And the unconscious mechanism of identification,[6] the transformation (seemingly not acknowledgeable and certainly therefore not owned by V) into the crazy, sadistic mother who lived on within V's psyche as a kind of succubus, made for a life of intermittent delusion—and also of course of misery—for everyone around her and for the split-off, nonmother, mother's victim part of herself.

5. It was once told to me, I believe by Max Schur, Freud's physician, that Freud once said in a discussion on sadism and masochism, "Those who are sorry are having their fun twice."

6. Both identification and projection are unconscious mechanisms and are inherently delusional. The attenuation of delusion can be accomplished only if the mechanisms can become conscious. The patient must be able to bear in consciousness—full, affect-laden consciousness—both the knowledge of what it feels like to identify with and project onto an other and the dangers attendant on this insight.

5

....

SAMUEL BUTLER,

A LITERARY

EXAMPLE

When we love, we draw what we love closer to us;
when we hate a thing, we fling it away from us. All
disruption and dissolution is a mode of hating; and
all that we call affinity is a mode of loving.
—Samuel Butler, *Notebooks*

I want to furnish a nonclinical illustration of everyday delusions—partly paranoid (and therefore, as I have stated, based on malignant envy) and also arising from identification with a similarly disturbed parent—drawn from the life and writings of Samuel Butler (1835–1902). Butler was not only, as the epigraph to the previous chapter would indicate, a proto-Kleinian, but also—see the epigraph to this chapter—a proto-Freudian. In *The Way of All Flesh*, published posthumously in 1903 but most of it written years before he could have heard of Freud (he did no revisions after 1884), he wrote,

> I fancy that there is some truth in the view which is being put forward nowadays, that it is our less conscious thoughts and our less conscious actions which mainly mould our lives and the lives of those who spring from us. (54)

Butler had a lifelong ambivalent attachment to his family, especially to his parents. He once wrote that if a biography of him were written, it ought to begin with the statement "The subject of this memoir was born of rich but dishonest parents. . . . He inherited the dishonesty, but not the wealth of his family" (1874–83, 288). Butler's hostility was most openly concentrated on his father (and the following note shows that his brother also had a considerable share):

MY MOST IMPLACABLE ENEMY from childhood onward has certainly been my father. I doubt whether I could not make a friend of my brother more easily than I could turn my father into a cordial, genial well wisher; and yet I do not for a moment doubt the goodness of his intentions from first to last. (1874–83, 222)

Butler's perceptive biographer, Peter Raby, alerted me to the sting in the tail of this note—"The apparent generosity of the concluding concession is momentary, lasting only until one recalls the traditional association of 'good intentions' " (1991, 23). Raby observes that "the full force of the struggle [between father and son] is expressed in a note, 'Family, Fable of the Erinyes'[1] which constructs a general principle from Butler's experience at Langar [the family home]:

> FAMILY, FABLE OF THE ERINYES The Ancients attached such special horror to murder of near relations because the temptation was felt on all *hands* to be so great that nothing short of this could stop people from laying violent *hands* upon them. The fable of the Erinyes was probably invented by fathers and mothers and uncles and aunts. (1874–83, 221; my italics)[2]

Raby's impression that this note, with its connotations of parricide, is relevant to the previously quoted one about father as enemy was made more convincing when I found that they both were written in the same month in 1883 (see Butler 1874–1902a, 221–22).

1. The Erinyes are the Furies who in Greek mythology avenge the murder of relatives.

2. Although Butler revised and edited his earlier notes in 1896, he retained the awkward iteration of "hands" in this one. Is this uncharacteristic infelicitous writing, one wonders, or an unconscious need to emphasize hands as an allusion to a sadomasochistic incestuous masturbation fantasy?

The hostile side of Butler's ambivalence toward the women in his family (openly expressed in his *Notebooks*) and toward women in general can be copiously documented. A lifelong bachelor, he wittily and mordantly expresses some of the almost somatic intensity of his misogyny (as well as displaying his antireligious bent) in a typical perversion of a well-known quotation—here from Lamentations 1:12:

> Behold and see if there be any happiness like unto the happiness of the devils when they found themselves cast out of Mary Magdalene. (1874–1902a, 228)

The Way of All Flesh, which Butler worked over for a good part of his adult life (he didn't want it published while members of his family were still alive), is a documentation of his impressions of his childhood.[3] His hero, Ernest Pontifex, is the firstborn son—as Samuel had been—of a wealthy clergyman, Theobald Pontifex, who is based on Butler's own father (*pontifex* is Latin for *priest*). He says of Ernest,

> Before Ernest could well crawl he was taught to kneel; before he could well speak he was taught to lisp the Lord's prayer, and the general confession. How was it possible that these things could be taught too early? If his attention flagged or his memory failed

3. Raby writes, "Samuel Butler recorded his childhood in *The Way of All Flesh.* Although it is not of course true in every particular, it is, both on his own and others' account, an extremely faithful record of actual events, incorporating with scrupulous care letters, inscriptions, topography, incidents. . . . If Thomas and Fanny Butler are on trial as Theobald and Christina Pontifex, as it often seems they are, then we hear very little in their defense. But the imaginative and emotional force of the novel makes it disturbingly convincing. Cowed and subjugated as a child, Samuel sustained an intense hurt, which he locked away until he was able to express some part of it in a manuscript that he once regarded as his *magnum opus*" (1991, 16).

him, here was an ill weed which would grow apace, unless it were plucked out immediately, and the only way to pluck it out was to whip him, or shut him up in a cupboard, or dock him of some of the small pleasures of childhood. Before he was three years old he could read and, after a fashion, write. Before he was four he was learning Latin, and could do rules of three sums. (1903, 95–96)

Children in Victorian England were frequently hounded into becoming submissive premature adults partly with the rationalized purpose of ridding them of their inherent sinfulness. Soul murder was easy to justify as a socially accepted, religiously righteous way of rearing children—institutionalized in the family; Charles Dickens's *Hard Times* and many of his other novels document this. Following in the path of the novels of Charlotte and Emily Brontë, George Eliot, and George Meredith and the autobiographies of J. S. Mill and Edmund Gosse, Samuel Butler's last novel is both a continuation and in some ways the culmination of protest in English literature against Victorian family dictatorship.

We all identify with, as well as react against, aspects of our parents' characters. These identifications are complex mixtures of positive and negative impressions, and their modification toward flexibility as the child matures is basic to the achievement of a separate identity. In the course of the never fully completed struggle to throw off our initial dependency on parents, we should gradually become able to turn to people other than parents as objects for emulation and interaction; these dependent ties also ought to become more flexible. If the parents are grossly paranoid, depressed, or schizophrenic, this will of course profoundly affect the children who identify with them—but not always in predictable ways, although disturbed and traumatizing parents inevitably evoke an increased need to hold on to them by identification.

Because the premise of this book involves the universal (although individually idiosyncratic) retention of delusions as a residue of the earliest mental functioning, it follows that the parents are not only potential sources of delusions and quasi-delusions by way of identification with them, but also (at least unconsciously) the object of the delusions (frequently disguised in displacement onto others). We are therefore persecuted by figures derived from the early bad primal parents. (As I have mentioned, they are the basic source of Satan, malevolent gods, and all the evil creatures associated with them in our myths and folklore and fantasies.)

The presence of a parent who, over and above possessing the delusions of everyday life, is extremely disturbed in relation to reality adds a powerful incentive to the tendency for the child toward psychotic ideas, defenses, attitudes, mechanisms. But these identifications with frankly psychotic parents do not in themselves create the (probably organically based) major psychotic illnesses. These, however, can be simulated. And if there is too much trauma or deprivation at the hands of the parents, the interferences with healthy development might very well in some instances result in psychoses, even if there are no inherited organic deficiencies or catastrophic early environmental disturbances other than those imposed by parental pathology.

The identification is not necessarily only with a parent who is paranoid in his or her attitudes and feelings but frequently also with one who has actually been a persecutor in action. In the Butler (and the Pontifex) family the father was repeating the persecution in relation to his child that he himself had experienced as the child of a persecuting parent.

Raby's excellent biography (1991) shows how much the domineering, controlling, disapproving, joy-depriving qualities that were there in Samuel Butler's father, Thomas, existed in Thomas's father as well (see Raby 1991, 18). In *The Way of All Flesh*, Theobald Pontifex's attitude toward his children is derived from his father's attitude toward him as a child:

> Theobald had never liked children. . . . [Things] might have been better if Theobald in his younger days had kicked more against his father: the fact that he had not done so encouraged him to expect the most implicit obedience from his own children. . . . No duty could be more important than that of teaching a child to obey its parents in all things. . . . The first signs of self-will must be carefully looked for, and plucked up by the roots at once before they have had time to grow. (1903, 116–17)

This passing down of the consequences of the sins of the father happens often. In the child's psychic registrations of actions, feelings, and thoughts, the paranoid delusionary tendencies (here as part of soul murder: see Shengold 1989) flow on from generation to generation. Butler wittily comments in a characteristically skewed paraphrase:

> How often do we not see children ruined through the virtues, real or supposed, of their parents. Truly He visiteth the virtues of the fathers upon the children unto the third and fourth generation. (Butler 1912, 25)[4]

In the novel Theobald—a recently married man, grown self-important now that he has acquired a worshipful wife whom he can bully—is described as regressing from his grandiose father-

---

4. I cannot forbear quoting a characteristic Butlerian misanthropic twisting of a cliché which overtly expresses his specific hatred of marriage and, indeed, of every kind of deep emotional attachment—but, more important, seems to me to express the essence of masochism:

'Tis better to have loved and lost
Than never to have lost at all.(1903, 370)

identification to helpless infancy whenever he approaches contact with his father:

> True—immediately on [Theobald's] arriving within a ten-mile radius of his father's house, an enchantment fell upon him, so that his knees waxed weak, his greatness departed, and he again felt himself like an overgrown baby under a perpetual cloud. (1903, 90)

Raby (1991) specifically links the association for Samuel "of learning with punishment" (19) as one passed down through the three generations. He quotes from a letter in which Thomas Butler's father, Bishop Samuel Butler, who was then headmaster of Shrewsbury School, wrote to a parent,

> Your son had been flogged twice, and twice only, when you saw him, and each time with neither more nor less than the usual degree of punishment, which consists of six cuts with a few twigs of loose birch held in the hand. . . . With regard to allowance being made for your son's backwardness, I have only to state that ample allowance has always been made for the backwardness of him and of every backward boy; but to great backwardness he joins great idleness, and it is necessary for any master who means to do his duty faithfully to a boy or his parents, to correct this when he sees fit. (Raby 1991, 18–19)

This "usual degree of punishment" prevailed in Victorian England's public schools. Raby adds, "Thomas Butler in his turn did his duty, and with . . . immoderation and insensitivity" (19). In *The Way of All Flesh*, Samuel (Ernest in the novel) writes, "When Ernest was in his second year, [his father] began to teach him to read. He began to whip him two days after he had begun to teach him" (1903, 98). The association of physical punishment with education continued when Samuel went to boarding school. Of the library of

"Dr. Skinner" (the novelistic equivalent of Dr. Kennedy, the head-master of Shrewsbury School when Butler was a student there), Butler writes,

> In the meantime Theobald and Ernest were with Dr. Skinner in his library—the room where new boys were examined and old ones had up for rebuke or chastisement. If the walls of that room could speak, what an account of blundering and capricious cruelty would they not bear witness to! (1903, 144)

In his novel, Butler furnishes the following recipe for crushing a child's separate identity and capacity for joy (soul murder). The novel's narrator ironically expresses the philosophy of child-rearing that motivated Ernest's (Samuel's) grandfather's bringing up of Ernest's father, Theobald—and that was repeated by Theobald in relation to Ernest:

> To parents who wish to lead a quiet life I would say: Tell your children that they are very naughty—much naughtier than most children. Point to the young people of some acquaintances as models of perfection and impress your own children with a deep sense of their inferiority. You carry so many more guns than they do that they cannot fight you. This is called moral influence, and it will enable you to bounce them as much as you please. They think you know and they will not have yet caught you lying ofen enough to suspect that you are not the unworldly and scrupulously truthful person which you represent yourself to be; nor yet will they know how great a coward you are, nor how soon you will run away, if they fight you with persistency and judgment. You keep the dice and throw them both for your children and yourself. Load them then, for you can easily manage to stop your children from examining them. Tell them how singularly indulgent you are; insist on the incalculable benefit you conferred upon them, firstly in bringing them into the world at all,

but more particularly in bringing them into it as your own children rather than anyone else's. Say that you have their highest interests at stake whenever you are out of temper and wish to make yourself unpleasant by way of balm to your soul. Harp much upon these highest interests. . . . You hold all the trump cards, or if you do not you can filch them; if you play them with anything like judgment you will find yourself heads of happy, united, God-fearing families. . . . True, your children will probably find out all about it someday, but not until too late to be of much service to them or inconvenience to yourself. (1903, 28–29)

Brainwashing is indicated here with poignant bitterness.

Soul murder and brainwashing are exemplified later in the book. Mr Overton, the narrator, is describing what he has witnessed. Ernest, as a small child, was trying to recite a hymn, "Come, come, come; come to the sunset tree":

[Ernest] was, however, very late in being able to sound a hard "c" or "k," and instead of saying "come," he said "Tum, tum, tum."

"Ernest," said Theobald, from the armchair in front of the fire where he was sitting with his hands folded before him, "don't you think it would be very nice if you were to say 'come' like other people, instead of 'tum'?"

Theobald was always in a bad temper on Sunday evening. . . . I had already seen signs that evening that my host was cross, and was a little nervous at hearing Ernest say so promptly, "I do say tum," when his papa had said he did not say it as he should.

Theobald noticed the fact that he was being contradicted in a moment. He got up from his armchair . . . "No, Ernest, you don't," he said, "you say nothing of the kind, you say 'tum,' not 'come.' Now say 'come' after me, as I do."

"Tum," said Ernest at once; "is that better?" I have no doubt he thought it was, but it was not.

"Now, Ernest, you are not taking pains; you are not trying as you ought to do. It is high time you learned to say 'come'; why Joey can say 'come,' can't you, Joey?"

"Yeth, I can," replied [cousin] Joey, and he said something which was not far off "come."

"There, Ernest, do you hear that? There's no difficulty about it, nor shadow of difficulty. Now, take your time, think about it, and say 'come' after me."

The boy remained silent a few seconds and then said "tum" again.

I laughed, but Theobald turned to me impatiently and said, "Please do not laugh, Overton; it will make the boy think it does not matter, and it matters a great deal"; then, turning to Ernest he said, "Now, Ernest, I will give you one more chance, and if you don't say 'come,' I shall know that you are self-willed and naughty."

He looked very angry, and a shade came over Ernest's face like that which comes upon the face of a puppy when it is being scolded without understanding why. The child saw well what was coming now, was frightened, and, of course, said "tum" once more.

"Very well, Ernest," said his father, catching him angrily by the shoulder. "I have done my best to save you, but if you will have it so, you will," and he lugged the little wretch, crying by anticipation, out of the room. A few minutes more and we could hear screams coming from the dining-room, across the hall which separated the drawing-room from the dining-room, and knew that poor Ernest was being beaten.

"I have sent him up to bed," said Theobald, as he returned to the drawing-room, "and now, Christina, I think we will have the servants in to prayers," and he rang the bell for them, red-handed as he was. (1903, 103–04)

The verses Theobald then recited began:

> But the soul that doeth aught presumptuously, whether he be born in the land or a stranger, the same reproacheth the Lord; and that soul shall be cut off from among his people.
>
> Because he hath despised the word of the Lord, and hath broken His commandments, that soul shall be utterly cut off; his iniquity shall be upon him.

[Then the Lord orders Moses to tell the people to put to death a man who has violated the Sabbath by gathering up sticks.]

> And all the congregation brought him without the camp, and stoned him with stones, and he died; as the Lord commanded Moses. (1903, 105)

Theobald, in his righteousness, invokes not only soul murder but literally murder. (I speculate that Butler here, perhaps unconsciously, is suggesting that his father also should be cast out and stoned for his "presumptuous" punishment of his child.)

So Samuel Butler certainly felt persecuted by his parents, above all by his father. And in his *Notebooks*, like *The Way of All Flesh* written over many years and published after his death, he expresses his hatred of both parents directly as well as of his siblings:

> MY FATHER AND MYSELF
>
> He never liked me, nor I him; from my earliest recollection I can call to mind no time when I did not fear him and dislike him; *over and over again I have relented toward him and said to myself he was a good fellow after all*; but I had hardly done so when he would again go for me in some way or other which soured me again. . . . *I am not at all sure that the fault is more his than mine.* (1874–83, 231; my italics)

I have underlined the denial, the need to negate the hostile impressions and expectations Samuel Butler felt (whether or not these were factually, "historically" justified; "the fault" would most probably have also at some point been taken onto himself by the boy—with the consequent establishment of a hostile provocative symbiotic tie—the boy's provocation then justifying the father's accusations). The masochistic need to deny "over and over again" shows how strongly Samuel craved a good father whom he could love and be loved by—a humiliating and frustrating need that Butler buried under the surface of provocative anger, reproach, and rebellion that only sometimes was in turn covered over by a polite and submissive obedience.

Greenacre writes,

> Butler's mother seemed to play a singularly meager role in his life, appearing rather as part of the "they," the parent who condemned him when he hungered for recognition and approval, but on his own terms. She was described by her second cousin, Mrs. Richard S. Garnett, as the "most devotedly obsequious wife in all England." (op. cit., 71)

(Actually Butler wrote that description of his mother himself—applying it to Christina, the mother of Ernest, in *The Way of All Flesh*—1903, 89).

I think Greenacre underrates the importance of Butler's mother here. For the most part Samuel regarded his Fanny Butler as an abettor and idealizer of his father. She apparently never supported her sons when they opposed or were oppressed by her husband. She was a religious woman and this too made for adherence to Canon Thomas Butler and his opinions (his word and God's were confounded). That Fanny is called Christina in *The Way of All Flesh* shows her religious connotations for her son. Samuel soon grew to distrust her seductive righteousness. She would induce the boy to confess and then betray him to his father to be punished. There is this poisonous description in *The Way of All Flesh*:

Christina did not remonstrate with Theobald concerning the severity of the tasks imposed upon their boy, nor yet as to the continual whippings that were found necessary at lesson times. Indeed, when during any absence of Theobald's the lessons were entrusted to her, she found to her sorrow that it was the only thing to do, and she did it no less effectually than Theobald himself; nevertheless she was fond of her boy, which Theobald never was, and it was long before she could destroy all affection for herself in the mind of her firstborn. But she persevered. (1903, 96)

Here, again, the venomous sting is in the tail.

Raby documents that the writings of others in the family paint a very different picture of Fanny Butler, and "her letters reveal an affectionate, humorous woman, secure in her well-ordered world of family and parish life" (1991, 21). We can also doubt whether the unrelieved villainy and hypocrisy of Samuel's father in his guise as Theobald Pontifex is historically entirely valid. One of Samuel Butler's nephews wrote a letter to Mrs. Richard Garnett (who was writing a book to counteract son Samuel's scathing and satiric depiction of Canon Thomas in *The Way of All Flesh*):

To understand something of the atmosphere of [the family home] which so strongly reacted on Uncle Sam, it is necessary to go back to the early life of his father. My grandfather had been brought up at Shrewsbury School, as a boy greatly in subjection to his father, the headmaster, later as a junior master under him, always under his eye and his control. He wished to go into the Navy, but was compelled by his father to take orders, and was appointed curate at . . . a small village about a mile from Shrewsbury [where] he was still under family control, for Archdeacon Bather, [the] vicar [there], had married his eldest sister. (quoted in Henderson 1954, 8)

The nephew goes on to say that the troubles caused Canon Butler by his son Samuel resulted in the canon's seeing "no way of dealing with the problem but by treating Uncle Sam as severely as he would have treated a recalcitrant boy at the school" (9).

Whatever the actuality of Thomas Butler's character, there can be no question that in his writings Samuel was documenting how his father was recorded in his mind.

Beneath Butler's hatred of his father—"Those who have never had a father can at any rate never know the sweets of losing one. To most men the death of his father is a new lease on life" (1874–1902b, 100)—there lies his perhaps even deeper hatred of his mother. I speculate that it is about her that he has the following memory or, most probably, fantasy:

> "Promise me solemnly," I said to her as she lay on what I believed to be her death bed, "if you find in the world beyond the grave that you can communicate with me—that there is some way in which you can make me aware of your continued existence— promise me solemnly that you will never, never avail yourself of it." She recovered and never, never forgave me. (1874–83, 283)

Butler's hatred of his siblings, specifically of his sisters, was partly envy—the sisters were approved of by the parents: "The parents and two daughters seemed to form a compact group— smug, righteous, and ready to apply their procrustean standards generally" (Greenacre 1963, 70).[5] From Butler's *Notebooks* (Butler was seriously interested in becoming a painter and a musician):

> One of my sisters' amenities is to call my painting "drawing." If I

5. "Butler's father and mother have achieved an unenviable immortality as Theobald and Christina Pontifex in *The Way of All Flesh*. His sisters' less amiable characteristics are reflected in Charlotte Pontifex in the same book" (Keynes and Hill, introduction to Butler 1874–1902b, 8).

say I am painting such and such a picture they reply that they are glad I am "getting on with my drawing"—they never call it painting; they know the difference very well, they don't make the mistake to Edith Hall; it is intended as a way of cheapening what I am doing. . . . Another trick that my elder sister has is, when I play her anything on the piano, to say, "Oh yes, yes, I can see that would be very nice"—meaning of course—"if it was properly played, but you play it so damned badly that I can only see it would be very nice." (1874–1902a, 244)

Butler's hatred for his brother was also partly in identification with his parents: his younger brother, Tom, was if anything even more hostile and provocative toward his bullying, righteous father than Samuel; and, toward the end of Tom's life, even more hated by their father—a hatred which Samuel shared. When Tom Butler, a ne'er-do-well, deserted his wife and children and took up with prostitutes, Samuel rather enthusiastically supported his father's outrage and disapproval. (Canon Butler even wrote that he would prefer it if Tom were dead.)

Samuel also wanted to be loved by his parents and his sisters (toward his brother there was a more unmixed hostility). His clumsy attempts to ingratiate himself were drowned out by his provocative and accusatory feelings, which, however much they were based on what was really there in the family, had a paranoid quality. Greenacre says,

[Butler's] attitude toward his parents was to become one of persistent bitterness, but with a profound longing for affection which paradoxically caused him to make the most provocative demands on them and then be outraged when they did not comply. (1963, 71)

Butler's attempt to separate from his parents, successful as it may appear superficially from the predominantly sarcastic and hostile tone of his written references to them, was never really accomplished. He constantly sought out his parents' and even his sisters' admiration for his paintings, music, and books—an admiration the rational side of him knew he would never get. His father never read any of his books. Greenacre (1963) comments,

> Even at the age of forty-seven he wrote that his father had never liked him, and that he could recall no time without fear and dislike on his side, too. The attachment was unending. If Butler believed himself tormented by his father, he could never give up tormenting himself with the thoughts of his disappointment. (71)

The struggle left him negatively tied to his parents, especially to his father[6] and to authority figures and institutions that represented them (Charles Darwin and the Church of England, for example). It was a bond of compulsive provocative masochism, and it existed alongside the more unconscious bond of identification. At times it approached or arrived at paranoia but frequently with a considerable realistic core.

The progress toward paranoia is apparent in Butler's relationship to Charles Darwin, whom he knew and whose son was his friend. Butler, fascinated by, and with his own ideas about, the great man's theories, starts as his admirer and subsequently becomes his detractor and accuser, ending in obsessive paranoid hatred. Darwin had been a contemporary at Cambridge of Samuel

---

6. Here is an excerpt from his *Notebooks,* written while Canon Butler was still alive, that shows both Butler's death wishes toward his father and his unconscious need to keep contact with him afterward: "PHONOGRAPH FOR A BAD SLEEPER. A bad sleeper should have a phonograph to lull him to rest by preaching, we will say, my father's sermons. If I survive my father I will keep some of his sermons for this purpose. The machine should be placed on a high shelf to imitate a pulpit" (1874–83, 266).

Butler's father, Thomas, and, like him, had gone to school under Thomas's father, Samuel. Darwin was therefore easily identified with Canon Butler. Butler late in his life wrote an idealizing book about his grandfather and namesake, Samuel Butler (after portraying him villainously, as it were through Canon Butler's eyes, in *The Way of All Flesh*). He had earlier written admiringly of Charles Darwin's grandfather, Erasmus. After some years of cordial acquaintance and enthusiastic adherence to Charles Darwin's views, Butler took a turn toward feeling persecuted by him:

> Presently [Butler] found himself angry and feeling cheated by Darwin, even as he had originally been by the Church and his parents. His anger found a justification in facts—events which were true but were hardly a basis for the accusations of scientific duplicity which he brought against the bewildered Darwin. (Greenacre 1963, 95)

Butler (in his second book on evolution, *Evolution Old and New* [1879]) charged Charles Darwin with plagiarizing his own grandfather, Erasmus Darwin, and made

> a further charge that Darwin had allowed quotations from Butler himself to be used in a book on Erasmus Darwin without acknowledging their source. There was a nucleus of truth in Butler's charge, but the situation was not of great moment and had not developed as part of deliberate evil intentions on Darwin's side; rather it had been a combination of probably unavoidable errors and some neurotically determined oversights [on Darwin's part]. Butler clearly found a toehold for his increasing hostility to Darwin and made the most of it until it developed into a paranoid attitude which he was never able to overcome. . . . The rancor and sense of grievance persisted throughout Butler's life, as his notes and letters show. (Greenacre 1963, 45–46, 95)

As Raby comments, Butler turned Darwin's "simple oversight [into a] far-fetched conspiracy theory" (1991, 174). Raby continues,

> The episode left Butler with a profound sense of injury at the hands of what he saw as the scientific establishment, in the person of Darwin and his followers, Huxley and Romanes. He pursued the vendetta remorselessly, penning lengthy and obsessive letters whenever the matter resurfaced in the public domain. . . . He also became absurdly jealous, scouring the writings of others for signs that they had used something of his without acknowledgement. (174)

In accordance with Freud's theory of paranoia, the longing for affection (with its unconscious sexual roots) from his father was turned into paranoid hatred displaced onto these figures from the "scientific establishment."

Raby quotes a letter Samuel sent to Frank Darwin shortly after the publication of Butler's first book on evolution, *Life and Habit*, in which he expressed apprehension about Charles Darwin's reactions to it:

> How sorry I was that your father should have been at school under my grandfather, inasmuch as I myself should dislike an attack from a *son* or *grandson* of my [schoolmaster's] when I should not care twopence about it from anyone else. (my italics)

There was an unconscious identification with his father in his gratuitously bringing in a son (his father) as well as, appropriately, a grandson (himself). Raby comments,

> In dragging in the family and two other generations, Butler was already beginning to exhibit symptoms of the paranoia that would infect all his dealings with Darwin and the scientists. (1991, 164)

Charles Darwin was confused about the reasons for Butler's hostility and actually frightened by its vehemence. Butler's paranoid reaction was definite but limited and contained—except in his writings. (Butler's book *Luck and Cunning* is full of snide, antagonistic allusions to Darwin.) Despite his war with the great scientist and his attributing the neglect of his own books and ideas on evolution to Darwin and his followers, Butler was able to remain good friends with Darwin's son Frank.

There was also an adaptive response to all this hostility in that Butler developed his own theory of evolution, based on Lamarck and Erasmus Darwin, and went on to write four books on evolution. (Although in *The Way of All Flesh* Samuel Butler was trying to illustrate his own Lamarckian brand of evolution—trying to portray how acquired characteristics are passed down in a family by heredity—no evolutionary theory is necessary to explain the experiential handing down from generation to generation of soul murder,[7] which the novel documents.)

Butler was a good hater, and he resembled his righteous and intolerant father more than he allowed himself to know. I repeat that I am describing Butler's psychic registration of his father as revealed in his *Notebooks* and, in fictional form, in *The Way of All Flesh*—where the hateful qualities are split up between the protagonist's father, Theobald Pontifex, and his paternal grandfather, George Pontifex. Both are persecutors of children.

In his *Notebooks,* Butler wrote,

ASSIMILATION AND PERSECUTION. We cannot get out of persecution: if we feel at all we must persecute something; the mere acts of feeding and growing are acts of persecution. Our aim should

7. From the *Notebooks:* "I had to steal my own birthright. I stole it, and was bitterly punished. But I saved my soul alive" (1874–1902a, 182).

be to persecute nothing but such things as are absolutely incapable of resisting us. (1874–83, 246)

This rationalizes his feelings of persecution into a universal characteristic (like the delusions of everyday life); the last statement shows his identification with his father as persecutor, and it applies to his own continuing persecution of Darwin, as well as of other current cultural favorites like Dickens and Felix Mendelssohn, in his notebooks after their deaths—that persecution (expressing malignant envy) representing both revenge against and identification with father and grandfather.[8]

It comes as no surprise that Samuel Butler, after almost automatically going along with his father's wishes, discovered (as Thomas had before him) that he did not want to become a clergyman and emulate his father and grandfather. Unlike the canon (and his counterpart Theobald), Samuel Butler was eventually able, after Cambridge, to defy his father enough to decide to become a sheep farmer in New Zealand. However, he gave up trying to become a painter or a musician when his father persistently disapproved and did not actually emigrate until he had negotiated his father's reluctant consent. The rebellion was partial. His was a divided soul, and the son's yearning to be loved by his father and compulsion to hold on to him by becoming him existed alongside his despising and trying to break with his father. (Butler wrote in both *The Way of All Flesh* and his *Notebooks* that his father did not like children. Of course neither did Butler himself.) However, he was able to make a success of his sheep-farming venture, and this appears to have helped effect some psychic separation.

8. He also continued to feel persecuted by Darwin: "I attacked the foundations of morality in *Erewhon,* and nobody cared two straws. I tore open the wounds of my Redeemer as he hung upon the Cross in *My Fair Haven,* and people rather liked it. But when I attacked Mr. Darwin they were up in arms in a moment" (1874–1902b, 167).

Before Samuel sailed, Thomas Butler gave his son two thousand pounds and promised him three thousand more; much controversy ensued about the eventual fulfillment of this promise. But Samuel Butler "never managed to sound grateful" (Raby 1991, 67). He also resented it when his father had his letters from New Zealand printed as a book. Raby says Butler's allegation that his father published the book, called *A First Year in Canterbury Settlement*, "without his permission . . . is only partially true. His father edited it, but he did send the proofs to New Zealand for correction and amendment" (90). The proofs were lost in a shipwreck.[9] This is an example of Butler's elaboration and exaggeration of his father's dictatorial qualities, as the father similarly elaborated and exaggerated his son's hostile and rebellious qualities.

Part of what was like the father in the son were the obsessive-compulsive character traits that often accompany and underlie paranoid tendencies. Henry Festing Jones, who became Butler's constant companion in the latter part of his life, writes in his biography of Butler,

If Samuel Butler resented the restrictions of his parents' demands, he reproduced them in the rigid, almost ritualistic arrangements of his personal life. Already in his early thirties he was living in monastic simplicity, with a schedule for rising, eating, brushing his hair a hundred strokes each morning, smoking a given number of cigarettes each day, and carefully rationing his time for painting, writing, and his music. (Jones 1919, 71–72)

9. Raby thinks that the terrible review of the book published in the *Canterbury Press* in 1863 ("It is crude and wholly destitute of method" [quoted by Raby, 91]) might have been written by Butler himself. It would have been typical of his sardonic humor and certainly would have discharged some hostility toward what he felt was his usurping father.

This indicates not only identification with his father's regimens but also his own need for obsessive-compulsive control and what I have called (Shengold 1988) <u>anal narcissistic defensiveness—the need to shut out threatening emotional intensities and relationships by preoccupations with order and money.</u>[10] Butler was given to taking parental (maternal as well as paternal) financial and even nursing care of a whole series of sometimes ungrateful son figures. (H. F. Jones was a principal but usually not an ungrateful one of these younger men.) This tendency was also an identificatory residue for Samuel Butler of his relationship with his parents.

Most of the emotional contacts and combats with his father concerned money and its relation to dependency and separation (unconsciously, this involved who was going to control the child's anal sphincter). After Butler finished Cambridge and was casting about to find a way of earning a living other than going into the Church, he thought of trying to become an artist, in defiance of his father's wishes. Their correspondence at this time (featuring a kind of wrestling over money) leads to one misunderstanding after another by both parties; it is "painful" (Raby 1991, 54) to read. Raby comments, "Money, never far from centre stage in the Butler family drama, assumed a dominant role" (60). It was to dominate the relationship with his father up to the time of Thomas's death (at age eighty in 1887), which finally made Butler financially independent in early middle age (age fifty-one). In the form of identificatory obsessive preoccupation, money dominated the relationship even after the father's death. Butler shows this in an entry to the *Notebooks*:

10. Re Butler's anality: "OFFSPRING. A man's waste tissue and excrementa are to a certain extent offspring. The molecules have a greater aptitude for organization for their having been connected with him" (1874–83, 261). This could be translated: "I am my parents' shit."

MOTTO FOR MYSELF. I should like "The search for money comes first; morality after cash" [Horace, Epistles, V, 53–54]. (1874–83, 360)

This could be linked with Butler's previously quoted ironic statement that, born of dishonest but wealthy parents, he had inherited their dishonesty but not their wealth. Of course the statement, like the motto (which might well have been the secret motto for Theobald Pontifex), reflects identification, not inheritance. In spite of the identification, there was a very real feeling of liberation after the death of his father. Raby writes, "Butler was truly revitalized by [his father's] death" (225).

There is much about Samuel Butler's sexual life that is not known,[11] and it has been the subject of much speculation. He was obviously capable of heterosexual functioning, but it is not clear how much pleasure he derived from it—his friends who wrote about this sometimes make his sexual activity sound more like a compulsion than a delight. He had a pattern of protective, almost motherly relationships with a series of younger men, usually taller and better looking than himself (as was his father); there is no evidence that these were overtly sexual.[12] The one that perhaps meant most to him was that with a slightly younger man he met in New Zealand, Charles Paine Pauli. Butler met him in 1863; Pauli

11. This is of course true of most human beings—the exceptions are those who write biographic sexual confessions (which are unreliable, like Rousseau's) and those who have been analyzed, the analyst being the only judge and potential but forbidden witness.

12. Both recent Butler biographers, Henderson and Raby, doubt that there was any overt homosexual activity in Butler's relations with a series of younger friends and protégés: "There is no hint of physical homosexuality in any of his notes or letters" (Raby 1991, 93). (Of course in nineteenth-century England, with its cruel antihomosexuality laws, one would not expect overt references in notes and letters.) No certainty is possible here.

was ill and told Butler that he wanted to go to London to consult physicians there. Butler paid for his passage to England, and they remained friends for thirty years. It was a very strange relationship, passionate and masochistic (although probably not sexual) on Butler's part, in which the younger man used, controlled, and sponged money from the older one. Butler gave Pauli thousands of pounds over three decades—money which for most of those years he could ill afford. When he finally became relatively wealthy after his father's death, Butler gave Pauli an allowance of two hundred pounds a year. After Pauli died, Butler discovered that Pauli had had many other sources of income and other patrons, whose relationships with him were a mystery. Pauli turned out to be far from destitute; he had left (to others) the considerable estate of nine thousand pounds, so that he had not needed the support he cadged from Butler, and in his will not only had made no provision for repaying Butler but made no mention of him. Butler understandably felt foolish and betrayed. He must have hated Pauli for this and yet found he had to forgive him (he could easily have identified with Pauli's ingratitude toward a father figure). Butler wrote of the recently deceased Pauli, in 1897,

He was such a fine handsome fellow, with such an attractive manner, that to me he seemed *everything* I should like myself to be, but knew very well that I was not. I knew myself to be plebeian in appearance and believed myself to be more plebeian in tastes than I probably in reality was; at any rate I knew that I was far from being all that I should wish myself either in body or in mind. (quoted by Raby 1991, 93; my italics)[13]

13. In *The Way of All Flesh*, Butler writes of Ernest Pontifex, Theobald and Christina's son, "Ernest . . . hated and despised himself for what he, as much as anyone else, believed to be his cowardice. He did not like the boys whom he thought like himself. His heroes were strong and vigorous, and the less they inclined towards him the more he worshipped them" (1902, 157).

I think the "everything" (with its narcissistic connotations) in this self-derogatory statement shows that the idealized Pauli was one of several men who represented to Butler both what he consciously wanted to be and, at least unconsciously, wanted to have or be had by sexually.

In 1898, when Butler was working on writings that connected him with his past, he wrote the following sonnet, which seems to be about himself and Pauli—with the relationship to Pauli quite romanticized. (Pauli is represented as being much more emotionally involved than he apparently was.) Butler entitled it "An Academic Exercise," which seems to suggest a conscious wish not to have it interpreted as autobiographical:

> We were two lovers standing sadly by
> While our two loves lay dead upon the ground;
> Each love had striven not to be first to die,
> But each was gashed with many a cruel wound.
> Said I: "Your love was false while mine was true."
> Aflood with tears, he cried: "It was not so,
> 'Twas your false love my true love falsely slew—
> For 'twas your false love that was the first to go."
> Thus did we stand and said no more for shame—
> Till I, seeing his cheek so wan and wet,
> Sobbed thus: "So be it; my love shall bear the blame;
> Let us inter them honorably." And yet
> I swear by all truth human and divine
> 'Twas his that in its death throes murdered mine.

If indeed this was memory or even fantasy about Pauli in which some mutual discussion of the relationship and its ending takes place, it certainly shows Butler as full of passion. That there was homosexual love in fantasy seems beyond doubt, although it could easily have been idealized in conscious thought with the frank sexuality remaining unconscious. Butler's preoccupation with intensely close friendship between two men led him to write about it in two books: his book on Shakespeare's sonnets, with its comments on the relationship between Shakespeare and "the onlie begetter of these insuing sonnets," Mr. W. H.,[14] and his translation of Homer's *Iliad,* with its portrayal of the relationship of Achilles and Patroclus. In *Shakespeare's Sonnets Reconsidered* Butler says,

> One word more. Fresh from the study of the other great work in which the love that passeth the love of women is portrayed as nowhere else save in the Sonnets, I cannot but be struck with the fact that it is in the two greatest of all poets that we find this subject treated with the greatest intensity of feeling. The marvel, however, is this; that whereas the love of Achilles for Patroclus depicted by the Greek poet is purely English, *absolutely without taint or alloy of any kind,* the love of the English poet for Mr. W. H. was, though only for a short time, more Greek than English. I cannot explain this.[15] (1899, 159; my italics for what seems to me to be protesting too much)

14. The sonnet I quoted above that probably concerns Pauli is obviously modeled on Shakespeare's.

15. Butler (1899) is criticizing those who wish to differentiate Mr. W. H. (the "onlie begetter") as the dedicatee of the sonnets from the man to whom most of the sonnets are addressed: "If the Sonnets had been lost, and nothing had remained to us but the title page and dedication, who would have doubted that our loss had consisted of certain sonnets by Shakespeare, which were mainly conversant about a Mr. W. H.—that is to say, either addressed to him directly or written for his delectation. . . . Admitting the title page to be correct, 'onlie begetter' would have been taken to mean that though *Shakespeare's brain was the womb wherein the Sonnets grew, the influence which had fecundated that brain had proceeded solely from Mr. W. H.*" (29; my italics).

Butler furthers Shakespeare's procreational body imagery here, and elsewhere in the book he insisted at length on the evocation of fertile sexual intercourse by the metaphor "onlie begetter" contra a commentator (and others that followed

The last sentence seems disingenuous. I would think Butler could have explained it quite well (although perhaps still inconclusively) if he had been as free to attack the sexual hypocrisy about homosexuality that infected him here as he was free in relation to so many other aspects of Victorian hypocrisy. He surely knew that "English" homosexuality was no more or less pure than Greek; the need to conceal it did not make it "purer." Oscar Wilde had sued the Marquis of Queensbury for libel in 1895, and we know from a letter to Jones that Butler was aware of this and of the trial that followed. Before the trial, he had written a poem of idealized love to Hans Faesch, a young Swiss student whom Jones had met in 1893 and who became a very close friend of both older men. Faesch had had a weak chest, and Butler was a kind of nurse as well as an adoptive father to him. Raby describes the parting of the three when the young man left England after several years to take a job in Singapore:

> It was a poignant farewell, with tears flowing freely from all three. The next day, Butler, convinced that he would never see Hans again, expressed his feelings in a long poem which he called "In Memoriam HRF: 14 February 1895." . . . It concludes:

The minutes have flown and he whom we loved is gone,
The like of whom we never again shall see.
The wind is heavy with snow and the sea rough,
He has a racking cough and his lungs are weak.
Hand in hand we watch the train as it glides
Out, out, out into the night.

---

him) who had declared "begetter" to mean simply the nonsexual "procurer" or "obtainer" (1899, 27, 32–40). (In the course of this book, as in some of his writings on Homerian scholars, Butler shows his characteristic destructive zest toward competitors—sometimes humorous, sometimes almost paranoid in its hostility— directed at rival commentators on the text.)

So take him in thy holy keeping, O Lord,
And guide him and guard him ever, and fare him well!
(1991, 254)

In a subsequent letter to Faesch, Butler wrote, "I feel as though I had lost an only son with no hope of another."[16] Butler asked Faesch to send him a lock of his hair so that Butler could wear it in a silver locket.

Raby describes Butler's reactions to the Wilde case:

> As the trials proceeded, the decision about "In Memoriam" became clear. "About the poem," he wrote to Hans, "which I consider to be the best thing I ever wrote [if this is as sincere as it sounds, it is another delusion], things have happened in England which make Jones and me decide not to publish it even anonymously." [a note on the letter in Butler's hand reads, "This means the trials of Oscar Wilde"] (1991, 261)

We learn from H. F. Jones (1919) (who, perhaps because of his long association as a younger man with Butler and especially in the

---

16. Raby: "Butler, while hoping that the climate would do Hans good, . . . had one 'last great favour' to ask of him. If he found he had made a serious mistake when he got to Singapore, 'then, my dear Hans, let me beseech you in the name of all the affection a dear father can bear to a very dear son, by the absurd, idiotic tears that you have wrung from me, by those we wrung from yourself, by the love which Jones bears you and which you bear towards him—if these things will not prevail with you nothing will—apply to me, and do so without delay in whatever way will ensure your getting the answer quickest which you will immediately receive—I mean draw on me at once for your passage money and necessary expenses and come home. . . . And now with every loving and affectionate thought which one man can think about another, believe me always from the bottom of my heart yours S. Butler' " (1991, 256). What a contrast here to Butler's own father; it seems a reversed, negative parental identification in which an idealized father emerges with generous, loving, and concerned feelings toward the separating son.

wake of "the trials of Oscar Wilde," seems to have been particularly eager to guard against any trace of homosexuality)[17] that Butler habitually frequented prostitutes,[18] a habit that probably started when he was at Cambridge and was continued in his frequent trips abroad—he alludes to visits to brothels in Italy in his *Notebooks*. Raby quotes Desmond MacCarthy, who knew Butler for many years:

> Butler was a man to whom continence was impossible. But he never fell in love with a woman; women representing a necessity for which he paid. . . . The sex instinct was unusually strong in him from boyhood to old age, and he canalized it in that prosaic way which some men adopt who dread emotional disturbance in their lives. (Raby 1991, 156)

When he was in his thirties Butler picked up a Frenchwoman of easy virtue on the street. He went to her regularly, once a week, until she died more than twenty years later. More details about the relationship than Jones furnished come from Butler's valet, Alfred Cathie,[19] who, as an old man, told them to an interviewer. Her

17. In *Shakespeare's Sonnets Reconsidered* (1899), published after all the publicity about Wilde that caused many homosexuals to go into exile for fear of prosecution, Butler referred to homosexual actions as "a leprous or cancerous taint" (112).

18. As I have mentioned, Samuel Butler shared his father's intense indignation with his brother, Thomas, for having deserted his wife and family to live with a Belgian prostitute. In *The Way of All Flesh*, he has Ernest marry (disastrously) a former prostitute; Butler, with characteristic contrariness, was on both his father's and his brother's side.

19. Cathie was another emotional protégé. Hired at twenty-two, after Butler's father died, he soon became indispensable. Butler described him as "half son, half nurse, always very dear friend and play-mate rather than work-fellow—in fact he is and has been for the last ten years my right hand" (quoted by Raby 1991, 250). Butler allowed Cathie to take care of all his practical affairs, took him along on

favors were shared with Jones, and there may have been other clients. Her name was Lucie Dumas, but both Butler and Jones distanced her by characteristically calling her Madame (perhaps thereby unconsciously evoking mother). She was apparently a nice person (Jones wrote that she had a heart of gold), and Butler was able, very gradually, to develop something of a personal relationship with her and was saddened by her death. Greenacre comments,

> It was only after he had known her for fifteen years that Butler allowed her to have his name and address. Then, in some ritualistic recognition of their long time together, he brought her to his rooms to have tea sometimes. His behavior is strangely like [that of] Pauli, who refused to give him his address but would lunch with him regularly. . . . [There was] a regularized relationship [set up] between Madame, Butler and Jones. According to [Alfred Cathie], Butler visited her each Wednesday, and Jones went on Tuesdays. Each gave her a pound a week, including holidays. (1963, 83)

The "regularized" sexual sharing with Jones, certainly an unconscious homosexual link, shows some of Butler's characteristic obsessiveness (here brought in perhaps in the need to control polymorphic—homosexual and heterosexual, masochistic and sadistic—sexual impulses).

The woman with whom the adult Butler was most deeply involved emotionally was Eliza Savage, an intelligent, sympathetic, slightly younger acquaintance Butler made in art school in 1867. They met irregularly but wrote letters to each other assiduously from 1871 to Miss Savage's death in 1885. (Butler somewhat ne-

---

some of his continental holidays, even permitted him to get married (he disliked his friends' marrying).

glected the prompt answering of her letters in the last few years before her death. He did not know that she was ill, but after she died he felt very guilty about what he characterizes as neglecting her during this time.) She was a kind of literary advisor for *The Way of All Flesh*—which he sent to her in batches as he was writing it. Her advice was excellent, and the first two-thirds or so of the book that she supervised is, almost all critics agree, the best part of the novel. Butler felt that she wanted him sexually and as a husband, but he could not respond with sexual feeling. Nevertheless his emotions and his conflicts were profoundly engaged by her.

He was greatly moved by her unexpected death following an operation that he was not even aware she was about to undergo. Raby writes,

> He felt it so deeply that he even unburdened himself to Harriet Bridges, the sister with whom he had perhaps least in common of all the members of his family. (1991, 211)

The letter:

> I received such a shock last night that I hardly know how to write. I have lost my friend Miss Savage whom you have often heard me speak of, and no words of mine can express how great this loss is. . . . When I first came to know her, nearly twenty years ago, she was lame and suffering from what I supposed to be hip-disease; the lameness constantly increased and of late I had seen that she walked with great difficulty. I have no doubt that the operation was in connection with this. I never knew any woman to approach her at once for brilliancy and goodness. She was the most heroically uncomplaining sufferer I ever met, and the most unselfish. It is not that I saw much of her—this I did not—but we were in constant communication and, happily, for the last ten years I have preserved everything that she wrote—and she wrote

nothing that was not worth preserving. It is out of the question that I can ever replace her. I have it in my power, and am thankful to think of this, to leave a memorial of her, traced chiefly by her own hand, which will show what manner of woman she was; but it is one which cannot possibly be made public till I have long followed her. [He did prepare a volume of their letters which was published many years after his death.] I had rather that you none of you alluded to this letter. [I feel this last must have been to protect himself from the pain of the expected withholding of the much longed-for empathy and sympathy he knew he would not receive from his family.] When I come down next I shall probably speak of her if I do so at all much as I have always done. But you none of you probably had any idea, and indeed cannot possibly have had any idea, how much I valued her. For the moment I am incapable of thinking of any other subject. (Butler 1841–86, 258–59)

He wrote a poem in a sketchbook shortly before his own death:

And now, though twenty years are come and gone
Since I beheld her, I behold her still . . .
Death bound me to her when he set me free.
(quoted by Raby 1991, 280)

Although he wrote that he should have married her and felt that he should have loved her, he could not. He was apparently subject to the common-enough "madonna-whore complex" (so often found in men unconsciously tied to their mothers) and found any sexual feeling toward the valued woman impossible (my "flesh rebels"—see sonnet below)—for the cravings of the flesh he took to prostitutes.

Butler wrote three sonnets about Eliza Savage toward the end of his life. The second reads,

And now, though twenty years are come and gone,
That little lame lady's face is with me still:
Never a day but what, on every one,
She dwells with me, as dwell she ever will.
She said she wished I knew not right from wrong.
It was not that; I knew and would have chosen
Wrong if I could, but in my own despite
Power to choose wrong in my chilled veins was frozen.
'Tis said that if a woman woo, no man
Should leave her till she have prevailed; and, true,
A man will yield for pity if he can,
But if *the flesh rebels* what can he do?
I could not. Hence I grieve my whole life long
The wrong I did, in that I did no wrong.
(Butler 1871–85, 373; my italics)

The last sonnet ends:

And here, alas! At any rate to me
She was an all too, too impossible she. (374)

But the weekly, eventually almost dutiful, carnal discharge at Madame's was quite possible.

In *The Way of All Flesh,* Butler's hostile picture of his father in all its ambivalent bitterness burns vibrantly—as it does in his *Notebooks* (with a flame that engulfs many other father figures of late Victorian times). In the novel we have several examples of the kind of twisted projection that infuses Butler's characterizations. In a passage deleted by the original editor of the novel, Butler writes about what he feels is an isolated failing in (his beloved) Handel's *Samson,* the great oratorio setting of Milton's *Samson Agonistes:*[20]

20. This is a rare criticism of Handel, Butler's musical idol since his boyhood; the idealization was, later in life, supplemented by identification—Butler wrote

[In] the air "How willing my paternal love," . . . Manoah, Samson's father, tells us how little Samson really has to suffer in being blind—inasmuch as he, Manoah, can see perfectly well. This, he avers, should be enough for Samson:

"Though wandering in the shades of night
While I have eyes, he needs no light." [The italics are Butler's.]

Exactly so: this is the British parent theory all over. No wonder Milton's daughters did not like him. . . . Handel has treated these two lines with the utmost pathos, and I have looked in vain for the slightest hint of his having smelt a rat anywhere in their vicinity. I suppose the explanation lies in the fact that he lost his own father when he was six years old, was independent at the age of fifteen, if not earlier, and never married—so that his ideas of family life were drawn mainly from what the poets told him about it. (437–38)

This is most unfair to Manoah, to Milton (who, as an established great, was Butler's natural enemy), and to Handel. Samuel Butler has transferred Canon Butler or at least Theobald Pontifex onto poor Manoah. Manoah's belief in God might well have facilitated the transference, but Milton depicts him as being intensely concerned for his son and—in such contrast to Canon Butler—ready to give his all to obtain his release:

Manoah. His ransom, if my whole inheritance
May compass it, shall willingly be paid
And numbered down: much rather I shall chuse
To live the poorest in my Tribe, then richest,

mock oratorios in a Handelian style. Most of Handel's work was ignored by the musical public, as Butler's books were by the reading public, and Butler was given to verbal and written fulminations about both neglects.

And he in that calamitous prison left.
No, I am fixt not to part hence without him.
For his redemption all my Patrimony,
If need be I am ready to forgo
And quit: *not wanting him I shall want nothing.*
(ll. 1476–84; my italics)

The chorus, moved, responds,

Fathers are wont to lay up for their Sons,
Thou for thy son are bent to lay out all;
Sons wont to nurse their Parent in old age,
Thou in old age car'st how to nurse thy Son
Made older then thy age through eye-sight lost. (ll. 1485–89)

After the blind Samson has destroyed the Philistines and himself by
pulling down the pillars of their temple, Milton has Manoah speak
what are perhaps the most moving lines in the great poem:

Come, come, no time for lamentation now,
Nor much more cause, Samson hath quit himself
Like Samson . . .
Nothing is here for tears, nothing to wail
Or knock the breast, no weakness, no contempt,
Dispraise or blame, nothing but well and fair,
And what may quiet us in a death so noble.
(ll. 1707–09, 1720–23)

In these sentiments Butler apparently finds (transfers, projects)
nothing but the father's insincerity and mere public show of caring.

In his *Notebooks,* this distorting paranoid paternal transference
transforms so many malignantly envied popular idols of the adult
Butler's time into hypocritical and undeserving villains. Two such

are Mendelssohn and Dickens, both of whom Butler despised.[21] Even Bach (revived and championed by Mendelssohn in the mid-nineteenth century), whose works Butler also played on the organ and whom he admired, is denigrated when compared to Butler's beloved and comparatively neglected Handel (with whom, as I have indicated, he obviously identified). Perhaps Bach was somewhat badly handled *because* Mendelssohn had successfully led his revival. Spectacularly successful rivals do evoke malignant envy, and Dickens was the most popular novelist, Mendelssohn the most popular musician of Butler's time. (Mendelssohn had even been piano teacher to Queen Victoria.) Butler did appear to have felt that the fame and success of these two fantasied rivals—he thought of himself as a musician as well as a writer—had been stolen from him. It was as if they, like Darwin, had taken from him the possibility of becoming a popular author himself; none of his books, after the early *Erewhon,* made any money in his lifetime, and Butler's fame was, for the most part, posthumous.[22]

Another instance of this kind of delusional misrepresentation concerns Dr. Kennedy, the head of Shrewsbury School when Sam-

21. A sampling of comments on Dickens and Mendelssohn: "DICKENS AND HANDEL. They buried Dickens in the very next grave cheek by jowl with Handel. It does not matter, but it pained me to think that people who could do this could become Deans of Westminster" (1874–1902b, 7). He is writing facetiously about a small Italian hotel: "The walls of the [hotel] are painted in fresco, with a check pattern like the late Lord Brougham's trousers, and there are also pictures. One represents Mendelssohn. He is not called Mendelssohn, but I know him by his legs. He is in the costume of a dandy of some five-and-forty years ago, is smoking a cigar and appears to be making an offer of marriage to his cook" (1874–1902a, 261).

22. Butler, after depreciating Raphael as undeservedly popular in the nineteenth century: "How, then, did Raffaelle get his reputation? It may be answered, how did Virgil get his? or Dante? or Bacon? or Plato? Or Mendelssohn? or a score of others who not only get the public ear but keep it sometimes for centuries?" (1874–1902a, 150).

uel Butler was a pupil there. In the novel, he is portrayed as "the famous Dr. Skinner of Roughborough [grammar school]" (138) and given a very individual malevolent portrait:

> Could it be expected to enter into the head of such a man as this that in reality he was making his money by corrupting youth; that it was his paid profession to make the worse appear the better reason in the eyes of those who were too young and inexperienced to be able to find him out . . . that he was a passionate half-turkey-cock half-gander of a man whose sallow, bilious face and hobble-gobble voice could scare the timid, but who would take to his heels readily enough if he were met firmly?[23] (1903, 148)

This is doubtless based on Butler's feelings about Dr. Kennedy. But it must be remembered that Samuel's father, Thomas, taught at Shrewsbury (under his own father, Samuel, who was then head) before the younger Samuel was born; and that in that novel it is said of Ernest that at Roughborough, "nevertheless, he was far from happy; Dr. Skinner was too much like his father" (155).

Again, one doubts that Dr. Kennedy was as bad as Butler makes him in his guise as Dr. Skinner. Other former schoolboys certainly disagreed with Butler angrily—of course they may have been idealizing. (Butler himself writes about Dr. Skinner's "admirers and

---

23. Butler adds this apostrophe: "O schoolmasters—if any of you read this book—bear in mind when any particularly timid drivelling urchin is brought by his papa into your study, and you treat him with the contempt which he deserves, and afterwards make his life a burden to him for years—bear in mind that it is exactly in the disguise of such a boy as this that your future chronicler will appear. Never see a wretched little heavy-eyed mite sitting on the edge of a chair against your study wall without saying to yourselves, 'perhaps this boy is he who, if I am not careful, will one day tell the world what manner of man I was'" (1903, 148). This is a warning to the fathers of this world.

supporters—among whom it is only fair to say that the greater number of the more promising boys were found" [1903, 219].) But for the father figures he came across Butler generally had a distorting, devaluating prejudice (that started with his own father), which is of course the negative other side of idealization.

The proper nouns provided in the novel for these schoolboy years are significant: *Rough*borough School—an echo of *Batters*by-on-the-Hill (the name Samuel Butler gave to the village of Langar, his father's clerical living, where the boy was born). Both names evoke the frequent beating of Samuel Butler as a child by his father[24]—noted by others as well as by Samuel himself—as well as the headmaster's beatings at Shrewsbury. And the name *Skinner* reminds the reader of the envious Apollo's horrible revenge on the presumptuous satyr flautist Marsyas—flaying him alive.[25]

Butler seems to have lived the last of his life fairly happily. He was able to continue to travel abroad and to finish the work he had planned—except for *The Way of All Flesh*. He wrote a sequel to his only commercially successful book, *Erewhon,* called *Erewhon Revisited*, which was published in 1901 with the help of his admirer George Bernard Shaw. It received the best critical notices Butler had had since the publication of *Erewhon* thirty years before. Butler died peacefully at his home in London in 1902.

I would like to illustrate the kind of vertical split in the mind that makes for delusions and their defensive equivalents—here an ex-

---

24. Both Samuel's father and Dr. Kennedy were beaters of boys. Butler writes of Theobald's early years of fatherhood, "After some years have gone by he hears his children their lessons, and the daily oft-repeated screams that issue from the study during the lesson hours tell their own horrible story over the house" (1903, 97).

25. Marsyas found the flute that Athena had invented but abandoned. His skill became so great that he challenged Apollo (who played the lyre) to a musical contest. When the god, predictably enough, won (as parents will, Butler would have said), he skinned and killed his pitifully inadequate rival.

ample of Butler's (as Ernest of *The Way of All Flesh*) split self (ego and superego) when he was a schoolboy:

> I have said more than once that [Ernest] believed in his own depravity; never was there a little mortal more ready to accept without cavil whatever he was told by those who were in authority over him; he thought, at least, that he believed it, for as yet he knew nothing of that other Ernest that dwelt within him, and was so much stronger and more real than the Ernest of which he was conscious. (1904, 158)

[Butler then puts the inarticulate struggle within the boy's mind into an intrapsychic dialogue in which the "real" Ernest—the one separable from his father—says,]

> You are surrounded on every side by lies which would deceive even the elect, if the elect were not generally so uncommonly wide awake; the self of which you are conscious, your reasoning and reflecting self, will believe these lies and bid you act in accordance with them. This conscious self of yours, Ernest, is a prig begotten of prigs and trained in priggishness; I will not allow it to shape your actions, though it will doubtless shape your words for many a year to come. Your Papa is not here to beat you now; this is a change in the conditions of your existence, and should be followed by changed actions. Obey me, your true self and things will go tolerably well with you, but only listen to that outward and visible old husk of yours which is called your father, and I will rend you in pieces even unto the third and fourth generation as one who has hated God: for I, Ernest, am the God who made you. (158–59)

Butler here shows his awareness of intrapsychic conflict both between superego and ego (conscience versus self) and within superego and ego (providing two competing versions of conscience and self). In a narcissistically delusional mode, part of him has become God and another (the father part) is Satan. (These are of course entirely reversible roles.)

The insight that was there in Butler as novelist was not always available to him in his everyday life, where his delusions flourished, as all of ours do.

6

....

DELUSIONS

INVOLVED

IN PERVERSIONS

AND IN

BEING IN LOVE

> No healthy person, it appears, can fail to make
> some addition that might be called perverse to the
> normal sexual aim; and the universality of the
> finding is in itself enough to show how
> inappropriate it is to use the word
> *perversion* as a term of reproach.
> —Freud, *Three Essays on the Theory of Sexuality*

Lee Grossman (1993), in a paper that presents much of what I am going to say in this chapter,[1] reminds us that Freud (1940, 204)

> distinguished between the defensive operations in neurosis and perversion. . . . In neurosis, the wish is renounced, disguised, or otherwise inhibited, out of respect for dangers perceived in reality, whereas in perversion, the perception of reality is altered, and the wish retained. (423)

Freud clearly states, Grossman adds, that the distinction is not absolute—most phenomena are compromises in which both wish fulfillments and defenses (including those interfering with the perception of reality) are represented. Grossman lists phenomena in which the abrogating of reality takes place; these varied manifesta-

---

1. Grossman presented his paper, "The Perverse Attitude towards Reality," at the spring 1993 meetings of the American Psychoanalytic Association. I also gave a paper there, "Narcissistic Delusions," based on chapter 2 of this book and therefore was unable to hear Grossman's paper, but I felt from reading an abstract of it that we were working in the same area. We exchanged our papers, and it turned out that I was right.

tions have one common connection: "When unpleasurable affect threatens, reality no longer has its compelling quality" (423).

More generally, I see that intense sexual arousal, perverse or not, like any emotional intensity that pushes toward overstimulation, but with its own particular qualities and force, involves an alteration of consciousness and potential internal conflicts which inevitably compromise the functioning and the inhibitory power of reality testing and of its inner "organ," the hypothetical metapsychological psychic structure that Freud calls the superego. ("A stiff prick has no conscience," as the popular saying goes.) The untamed intensity of instinctual drives gives bodily impulses and feelings and wishes that have not been much modified in their derivation from them a perfervid, compelling quality that partakes of the paradise-or-hell, all-or-nothing nature of primitive psychic functioning. It is the clinging to infantile (narcissistic) roots that gives all sexuality, although perhaps especially what we call perverse sexuality, a delusional quality.

Referring to childhood sexuality, Freud (1905) wrote,

The conclusion now presents itself to us that there is something innate lying behind the perversions but that it is something innate in *everyone*, though as a disposition it may vary in its intensity and may be increased by the influence of actual life. What is in question are the innate constitutional roots of the sexual instinct. In one class of cases (the perversions) these roots may grow into the actual vehicles of sexual activity; in others they may be submitted to an insufficient suppression (repression) and thus be able in a roundabout way to attract a considerable proportion of sexual energy to themselves as symptoms; while in the most favourable cases, which lie between these two extremes, they may by means of effective restriction and other kinds of modification bring about what is known as normal sexual life. (171–72)

The "healthy person," who, according to Freud, inevitably has some perverse quality to his or her sexuality, is, then, toward one end of a spectrum that extends to those whose sexuality is dominated by exigent pregenital perverse wishes, feelings, impulses, aims, and practices. The (frequently) absolute compulsive quality of the masturbation of puberty, a time of the biological renewal of primal sexual drives, again shows the intensity of the early imbalance between drive and defense. Freud, in a prescient sentence in a letter to Fliess of 1897, writes,

> Masturbation is . . . the 'primary addiction,' and it is only as a substitute and replacement for it that the other addictions—to alcohol, morphine, tobacco and the like—come into existence. (1887–1904, 287)

(One would today stress that the truth of this statement depends on the presence of the preoedipal [primal and therefore inherently perverse] fantasies from early childhood that accompany the masturbatory action even into later life.) Elsewhere Freud says, "The sexuality of neurotics[2] has remained in, or been brought back to, an infantile state" (1905, 172). And of course we are all, at the very least, neurotic.

To crave something with a terrible intensity can easily lead to the stretching or even abrogation of reality considerations—to delusion or quasi-delusion. But Charles Brenner has convinced us that

2. This was written at a time when Freud did not yet see clearly that neurosis was inevitable and in that sense "normal" and that "healthy" and "normal" could not simply be equated any more than can "neurotic" and "pathological." The nineteenth-century assumption was that we, the doctors and ordinary people, were normal and they, the patients, were sick. Freud's "Civilisation and its Discontents" showed those who did not already know it that we are all, at the least, neurotic; but the discoveries at the beginning of the twentieth century of childhood sexuality and the Oedipus complex clearly foreshadowed this generalization.

compromise is omnipresent. Perverse impulses are imbued with defensive purpose, alongside strivings for gratification. Sometimes it is the need to escape danger rather than the compelling wish for gratification that is predominant in the break with reality and delusional functioning. This seems clearly true, for example, in fetishism, where the denial of castration seems to be such a dominant motivation. L. Grossman uses the phrase (apparently quoting a patient) "turning down the volume on reality." He applies it to a patient who directed this assault on the perception of reality, not in relation to the perverse impulses he gratified but toward the idea of the realistic consequences of those impulses. I think this is quite common, and not only in perversions: the stiff prick that has no conscience avoids knowledge of consequences, moral and realistic.

Dickens and Balzac are sometimes criticized for the one-dimensionality of their characters—E. M. Forster calls them flat in contrast to the round characters of Shakespeare and Tolstoy. Of course it must be remembered that we tend to take for granted what other people are like. It is generally a preconscious operation—assuming that we know them, defensively denying that human beings are constantly changing, and thereby disregarding the contradictory, complicating, and threatening aspects of others, especially those that reflect ourselves. Indeed, this automatic yet shallow recognition of a defined, unidimensional "person" as a familiar character (fixed once and for all, as if in a play constantly reread) applies above all to preconscious assumptions when thinking of oneself. Taking for granted that one's identity is definitively known is a defensive, quasi-delusional operation: it diminishes awareness of the passage of time and distances death. Besides, such ordinary simple-mindedness makes life easier, less demanding; and, more important, it makes us less likely to allow into consciousness repressed or suppressed shameful, guilt-ridden, unwanted, and dangerous aspects of our mental pictures of ourselves. We tend to cover these over by emphasizing surface appearance (frequently idealized and made younger)—making for a one-dimensional, flat presentation.

This reduction (with or without idealization and/or devaluation) is even easier to accomplish when dealing with strangers. There is even more automatic diminution of the complexities of human identity in considering people in the mass, especially those who are clearly not like us—alien beings: those of other religious or sexual persuasions, those whose nationality or skin color is different—basically those who unconsciously represent, by matching opposite qualities (like negatives of a photograph), our parents and ourselves. We easily treat strangers, especially those we simply read about or hear about, with automatic prejudice (positive as well as negative)—reducing the individual to a category that evokes emotional bias. And these prejudices too are quasi-delusional if not delusional operations that we not always are aware of or feel responsible for.

But there are people who do live like caricatures—especially some of those who were deficiently endowed at birth or who have been traumatized (usually as children) and have had to diminish their own humanity in order to control their too powerful, aggressively charged drives, emotions, and impulses. This defensive self-reduction (see Shengold 1988) is always hedged by denial and delusion of characterological compulsive force. In the opposite direction, there are people who are driven by what appears on the surface to be one or a few instinctually derived wishes of overwhelming intensity. These can be predominantly perverse sexual or predominantly aggressive wishes (fueled by envy, ambition, a drive for power, or for murder). These urgencies are obviously narcissistic in that the feelings of other people are ignored in a push for fulfillment; such motivations also involve primal mental representations of the parents (directly or in transference to good or bad parental substitutes), who can still be partly felt as parts of the self. These wishes have the appearance of simple drives but represent more complex agglomerates of wishes and defenses that have preserved or reattained qualities and intensities from the infantile period of life. Being narcissistic, the motivations most frequently (but not always consciously or at least obviously) are directed toward narcissistic mental representations: we want to be or to have the breast, the primal parent, and later the early mother and father and then other parental substitutes onto whom these earlier "objects"[3] of the wishes are transferred. The instinctual wishes become, to use psychoanalytic jargon, object-related (still retaining some, optimally less and less, of their earlier narcissistic qualities, which can increase with regression). The object of these later motivations is sometimes the parents directly, sometimes those who substitute for them. On our road to being able to love others we start with our parents; what begins narcissistically should become less so as we mature.

It is to be remembered, and Freud has reminded us, that being and especially falling in love is frequently delusional (and in part, for some in large part, remains a narcissistic involvement). In "On Narcissism: An Introduction," Freud presents falling and being in love as a narcissistic regression: "Being in love . . . has the power to remove repressions and reinstate perversions. It exalts the sexual object into a sexual ideal" (1914, 100). The presence of delusion is implicit in both statements. In a later work (1921) Freud extends

3. The instinctual drives are directed at an "object" that will serve to discharge or fulfill them. Objects can be and initially are narcissistic (part of the self-image) and gradually become separated out into "object representations" that are differentiated from the "self representations" of the mind. To see the other fully and separately (an achievement of mental maturity) is to be "object-related" (potentially caring and loving) and not narcissistic.

the first statement about the effect of being in love on the ego and especially the conscience (superego and ego ideal):

> The functions allotted to the [superego] entirely cease to operate. The criticism exercised by that agency is silent; everything that the object does and asks for is right and blameless. Conscience has no application to anything that is done for the sake of the object; in the blindness of love remorselessness is carried to the pitch of crime. (1921, 113)

Freud, in the same work, writes about the lover's overvaluation of the beloved:

> The tendency which falsifies judgement in this respect is that of *idealization*. But now it is easier for us to find our bearings. We see that the object is being treated in the same way as our own ego, so that when we are in love a considerable amount of narcissistic libido overflows on to the object.

[Freud is saying that when one falls in love, the falsified idealization of oneself that is part of narcissistic grandiosity gets projected onto the mental picture of the beloved.]

> It is even obvious, in many forms of love-choice, that the object serves as a substitute for some unattained ego ideal of our own.

[The ego ideal is derived first of all from the earliest narcissistic images of the parents.]

> We love [the beloved] on account of the perfections which we have striven to reach for our own ego, and which we should now like to procure in this roundabout way as a means of satisfying our narcissism. . . . The object has, so to speak, consumed the ego.

[Freud is describing love that is predominantly narcissistic and delusional in contrast to the more reciprocal (more object-related) loving and being loved in return that replenishes as well as depletes the ego.] However, he adds,

> Traits of humility, of the limitation of narcissism, and of self-injury occur in every case of being in love. (112–13)

The narcissistic depletion of self-esteem, with its concomitant delusional qualities, is seen in Romeo's initial intense but transient fascination with the rejecting Rosaline, which precedes the more reciprocal and lasting, more mature but still delusional love for her cousin Juliet.

At the start of the play, Romeo, speaking of Rosaline to Benvolio, tells him he is "out of her favour, where I am in love" (I:i:75). He calls his love "a madness most discrete" (I:i:199) and says that despite his rejection by Rosaline he is "stricken blind" to others and is unable to forget her. Benvolio, also paying tribute to delusion, asks, "Romeo, art thou mad?" (I:ii:54). Romeo replies,

> Not mad, but bound more than a madman is;
> Shut up in prison, kept without my food,
> Whipp'd and tormented . . . (I:ii:55–57)

Benvolio bids Romeo to come with him, masked, to the feast of the Capulets that night, where

> Sups the fair Rosaline, whom thou so lov'st,
> With all the admired beauties of Verona;
> Go thither, and, with unattainted eye
> Compare her face with some that I shall show,
> And I will make you think your swan *a crow*.
> (I:ii:88–92; my italics)

Romeo expresses his love in extravagant poetic language:

> ROMEO. When the devout religion of mine eye
> Maintains such falsehood, then turn tears to fires!

And these, who often drown'd could never die,
Transparent heretics, be burnt for liars!
One fairer than my love! the all-seeing sun
Ne'er saw her match since first the world begun.
BENVOLIO. Tut! you saw her fair, none else being by,
Herself poised with herself in either eye;
But in that crystal scales let there be weigh'd
Your lady's love against some other maid
That I will show you shining at this feast,
And she shall scant show well that now shows best.
ROMEO. I'll go along no such sight to be shown,
But to rejoice in splendour of mine own. (I:ii:93–106)

And, of course, with the first glance at Juliet, delusion is transferred
to her, and as predicted Rosaline is transformed from swan to
crow. Here grandiloquent bombast becomes direct and true poetic
metaphor. Romeo asks a servant,

What lady is that which doth enrich the hand
Of yonder knight?
SERVANT. I know not, sir.
ROMEO. O! she doth teach the torches to burn bright.
It seems she hangs upon the cheek of night
Like a rich jewel in an Ethiops ear;
Beauty too rich for use, for earth too dear!
So shows a snowy dove trooping with *crows,*
As yonder lady o'er her fellows shows.
The measure done, I'll watch her place of stand,
And, touching hers, make blessed my rude hand.
Did my heart love till now? forswear it, sight!
For I ne'er saw true beauty till this night.
(I:v:44–57; my italics)

Not even the magic potion that Puck applies to the eyelids of the lovers in *A Midsummer Night's Dream* works more quickly to abolish the old love and establish the new than this first sighting of Juliet does for Romeo. It is magical, and magic means delusion. (Note how, throughout what I have quoted, Shakespeare shows love-delusion arrived at through sight—through idealizing illusion if not hallucination of the beloved.) That delusion is of course only enhanced when Juliet, also instantly struck, allows and responds to Romeo's kiss, and reciprocal, grown-up, real love begins.

No one should know the delusional nature of love more thoroughly than someone who has been involved in a psychoanalysis, whether as patient or analyst, who soon discovers the delusional quality of transference and transference-love (as well as of resistance). Freud, who felt that *he* was a crow and not a swan, wondered how young, pretty women patients could fall in love so suddenly and deeply with a not particularly attractive middle-aged man like himself, who made no effort to be charming or seductive. His answer was transference of narcissistic, parental love from childhood with its inherent delusional nature. Because transference and the defensive operations that underlie what we call resistance in psychoanalysis operate in life as well as in therapy, we all, then, can and do behave, at least temporarily, in an obsessed, delusional manner in the course of our loves and in the course of our hatreds.

I return to the theme of people who can be transformed for us mentally into caricatures by the extreme emotional investment we make in them, giving rise to oversimplified impressions that begin "at first sight" as instantly transferred narcissistic love or hate. To complement this (and the still near-delusional but usually more realistically based phenomena of more lasting hate and love—like Romeo's and Juliet's), people do exist who impress us in a more permanent and overall fashion, viewed from the outside, at least, as being (and who may actually be) like some of the flat fictional characters of Dickens and Balzac.[4] They are living caricatures.

Dickens's Mrs. Jellyby is introduced in a chapter of his novel *Bleak House* entitled "Telescopic Philanthropy." Dickens shows her to us as if she were a fixed specimen, the personification of a certain type of philanthropic woman. At the same time, Mrs. Jellyby is depicted as looking through a telescope in her mind's eye, as it were, at the unfortunate Africans who are the objects of her charity. In being so occupied, she is unable and perhaps unwilling to see their individuality. She concomitantly completely ignores the individuality of her children and what is happening to them in her home (her own darkest Africa). Narcissism reigns in her philanthropy. She is introduced as a potential landlady for the night for the novel's heroine, Esther Summerson, and her cousins Richard and Ada. The three young people have been invited to stay at Bleak House but it is not yet ready to receive them. Mr. Kenge, a lawyer for Mr. Jarndyce, the owner of Bleak House, says,

> In-deed! Mrs. Jellyby is a lady of very remarkable strength of character who devotes herself entirely to the public. She has devoted herself to an extensive variety of public subjects, and is at present devoted to the subject of Africa, with a view to the general cultivation of the coffee-berry—*and* the natives—and the happy settlement on the banks of the African rivers of our super-abundant home population. (1853, 25)

When the young people arrive at the Jellyby home, they find a crowd. As Mr. Guppy, the lawyer's clerk who is accompanying

---

4. In Balzac's *Eugénie Grandet*, the heroine's father, Père Grandet, is more or less a living embodiment of avarice. It is seemingly his only passionate drive, and he is willing to sacrifice the welfare of his wife and child to its fulfillment. It has all the intensity of a sexual perversion; the rest of the world—the context, as Harold Bloom puts it—is "burned away" by such intensity.

them, puts it, "One of the young Jellybys been and got his head through the area railings. . . . The young Jellybys are always up to something" (1853, 26).

Esther gets out of the coach and makes her way through the crowd to help the child. As she narrates the episode, the boy was

> one of the dirtiest little unfortunates I ever saw, and [I] found him, very hot and frightened and crying loudly, fixed by the neck between two iron railings while a milkman and a beadle, with the kindest intentions possible, were endeavouring to drag him back by the legs, under a general impression that his skull was compressible by these means. As I found (after pacifying him) that he was a little boy with a naturally large head, I thought that perhaps where his head could go, his body could follow, and mentioned that the best mode of extrication might be to push him forward. This was so favourably received by the milkman and the beadle that he would immediately have been pushed into the area if I had not held his pinafore while Richard and Mr. Guppy ran down through the kitchen, to catch him when he should be released. At last he was happily got down without any accident. (26–27)

With all the noise this incident had caused, Esther assumed that Mrs. Jellyby was not at home, an impression reinforced when she passed "several more children on the way up [the stairs], whom it was difficult to avoid treading on in the dark." But Mrs. Jellyby was at home,

> and as we came into [her] presence, one of the poor little things fell downstairs, down a whole flight (as it sounded to me)—with a great noise.
>
> Mrs. Jellyby, whose face reflected none of the uneasiness which we could not help showing in our own faces as the dear child's head recorded its passage with a bump on every stair—

Richard afterwards said he counted seven, besides one on the landing—received us with perfect equanimity. She was a pretty, very diminutive, plump woman of from forty to fifty, with handsome eyes, though they had a curious habit of seeming to look a long way off. As if—I am quoting Richard again—they could see nothing nearer than Africa! . . . We expressed our acknowledgments, and sat down behind the door, where there was a lame invalid of a sofa. Mrs. Jellyby had very good hair, but was too much occupied with her African duties to brush it. The shawl in which she had been loosely muffled dropped on to her chair when she advanced to us, and as she turned to resume her seat, we could not help noticing that her dress didn't nearly meet up the back.

The room, which was strewn with papers and nearly filled by a great writing-table covered with similar litter, was, I must say, not only very untidy, but very dirty. We were obliged to take notice of that with our sense of sight even while with our sense of hearing we followed the poor child who had tumbled downstairs. . . . "You find me, my dears," said Mrs. Jellyby, snuffing the two great office candles in tin candlesticks which made the room taste strongly of hot tallow, "as usual, very busy; but that you will excuse. The African project at present employs my whole time. It involves me in correspondence with public bodies, and with private individuals anxious for the welfare of their species, all over the country. I am happy to say it is advancing. We hope by this time next year to have from a hundred and fifty to two hundred healthy families cultivating coffee and educating the natives of Borrioboola-Gha, on the left bank of the Niger." (27–28)

After what might have been "an excellent dinner if it had had any cooking to speak of" (31),

Mrs. Jellyby, sitting in quite a nest of waste paper, drank coffee all the evening, and dictated at intervals to her eldest daughter. She also held a discussion . . . of which the subject seemed to be—if I understood it—the Brotherhood of Humanity, and gave utterance to some beautiful sentiments. I was not so attentive an auditor as I might have wished to be, however, for Peepy [the boy who had fallen down the stairs] and the other children came flocking about Ada and me in a corner of the drawing-room to ask for another story; so we sat down among them, and told them in whispers Puss in Boots, and I don't know what else, until Mrs. Jellyby, accidentally remembering them, sent them to bed. As Peepy cried for me to take him to bed, I carried him upstairs. On my return downstairs, I felt that Mrs. Jellyby looked down upon me rather, for being so frivolous. It was nearly midnight before we found an opportunity of going to bed, and even then we left Mrs. Jellyby among her papers drinking coffee, and Miss [Caddy] Jellyby biting the feather of her pen. (32)

And there is Mrs. Jellyby. She never changes but continues to ignore her children and to be obsessed with her African project whenever she reappears in the novel. When her daughter Caddy tells her she is engaged and asks her permission to marry, she barely listens and responds only by reproaching her for not being more involved in the affairs of Borrioboola-Gha:

"Now, if my public duties were not a favourite child to me, if I were not occupied with large measures on a vast scale, these petty details might grieve me very much. . . . But can I permit the film of a silly proceeding on the part of Caddy (from whom I expect nothing else) to interpose between me and the great African continent: No. No," repeated Mrs. Jellyby, in a calm clear voice, and with an agreeable smile, as she opened more letters and sorted them. "No, indeed." (212)

She is of course a caricature, and Dickens is rightly reproached by critics for the one-dimensionality of so many of his characters. But people like Mrs. Jellyby do exist—obsessive-compulsive and sometimes paranoid characters with their humanity flattened by defense and delusion.

We don't know much about how Père Goriot and Mrs. Jellyby came to be so monstrous and predictable. From the study of patients and the victims of war and totalitarianism in the twentieth century, we have learned that dehumanization can result from inborn deficiencies and from defensive reactions to chronic and brutal trauma. The primal defenses of idealization and devaluation from the earliest period of development (evoked by birth defects or imposed by reaction to overwhelming traumatic neglect or overstimulation) can, especially in children, become involved in compulsive defensive repetitions that give rise to obsessive character distortions in an attempt (not always successful—the survival of the young Jellybys is constantly in doubt) to ward off the too-muchness of unmodified primal emotions. I am implying that on some unconscious level of her mind Mrs. Jellyby is identified with the children—both the abstract African "children" and her own—and also with their persecutors and enslavers. In this delusion-ridden split in her responsible awareness she is simultaneously trying to protect and murder them—but all the related emotional intensities have been distorted, displaced, or eliminated from consciousness by narcissistic regression.

Narcissistic intensities involving primal love and hate like those manifest in Mrs. Jellyby and in sexual perversions require either discharge in action or massive inhibition and defensive falsification or even extinction of emotions—along with denial, a delusional break with reality. Both the inner psychic world and the external world are falsified in the mind. And each of us has some share of obsessive-compulsive constrictive inhibition and of sexual perversion.

7

....

"OWNING"

AND ITS

THERAPEUTIC

IMPLICATIONS

The fact is that you must catch your thief before
you can hang him, and that it requires some
expenditure of labour to *get securely hold of* the
pathological structure at the destruction of which
the treatment is aimed. (my italics)
—Freud, *Analysis of a Phobia in a Five-Year-Old Boy*

Samuel Butler describes an instance of not "owning" in relation to
his father, who as noted is fictionalized as Theobald Pontifex in *The
Way of All Flesh*. Butler says of Theobald's attitude toward his
parish duties, such as trying to comfort and reassure dying parish-
ioners, "He does not like this branch of his profession—indeed he
hated it—but will not admit it to himself. The habit of not admitting things to himself has become a confirmed one with him"
(1903, 96). "Not admitting things" can range from conscious lying
to delusion. What is basic here is the disowning of one's feelings—
the road to inauthenticity. The frequently associated denial of external reality can amplify the diminution or break in one's sense of
identity.

There is a scene relevant to owning in the fourth act of Shakespeare's *Macbeth*. Macduff has come to England to seek out Malcolm, the son and rightful heir of King Duncan, whom Macbeth
has murdered. Malcolm first melodramatically falsely confesses
that he himself is even more evil than Macbeth. When Macduff
curses him, Malcolm renounces what he said, describing it as a test
of Macduff's honesty. He appoints Macduff to head his troops in
the forthcoming effort to unseat Macbeth. They are interrupted by
a relative of Macduff, Rosse, newly arrived from Scotland. He has
terrible news for Macduff:

ROSSE. . . . words . . .
That would be howl'd out in the desert air,
Where hearing would not latch them . . .
Let not your ears despise my tongue for ever,
Which shall possess them with the heaviest sound
That ever yet they heard.
MACDUFF.   Humh! I guess at it.
ROSSE. Your castle is surpris'd; your wife and babes
Savagely slaughter'd. To relate the manner
Were on the quarry of these murther'd deer
To add the death of you.
MALCOLM.   Merciful heaven!
What, man, ne'er pull your hat upon your brows;
Give sorrow words. The grief that does not speak
Whispers the o'er fraught heart, and bids it break.
MACDUFF. My children too?
ROSSE.   Wife, children, servants, all
That could be found.
MACDUFF.   And I must be from thence!
My wife kill'd too?
ROSSE. I have said.
MALCOLM.   Be comforted.
Let's make us med'cines of our great revenge
To cure this deadly grief.
MACDUFF. He has no children. All my pretty ones:
Did you say all? O hell-kite! All?
What, all my pretty chickens, and their dam,
At one fell swoop?
MALCOLM. Dispute it like a man.
MACDUFF.   I shall do so;
But I must also feel it as a man. (my italics)

[Macduff at first cannot accept what has happened. He tries to deny his loss with his desperate questioning. The well-meaning but emotionally shallow and puerile Malcolm bids Macduff speak—to give lip service to his feeling. But the *man* Macduff knows he must first feel fully ("as a man") before he can own his feelings and what has happened to evoke them. He continues,]

> MACDUFF. I cannot but remember such things were,
> That were most precious to me. Did heaven look on,
> And would not take their part? Sinful Macduff,
> They were all strook for thee! Naught that I am,
> Not for their own demerits but for mine,
> Fell slaughter on their souls. Heaven rest them now.
> MALCOLM. Be this the whetstone of your sword, let grief
> Convert to anger; blunt not the heart, enrage it.
> MACDUFF. O I could play the woman with mine eyes,
> And braggart with my tongue! But, gentle heavens,
> Cut short all intermission. Front to front
> Bring thou this fiend of Scotland and myself
> Within my sword's length set him if he scape,
> Heaven forgive him too. (IV:iii:193–235)

In the course of psychoanalytic treatment, the patient's defenses not only against superficial knowing but against the flow of feeling that makes for knowing in its deepest sense must be modified. That defensive modification makes it possible to own what one feels, what one is, and what one has been. *Owning* in this sense grants a sense of identity.

Not owning is brought about by many defensive operations; delusion is only one but perhaps the most effective way of achieving it. There is probably always some delusional element in the defense of denial, perhaps a result of such complex defensive maneuvers as isolation, repression, or negation (each person having his own dynamic and shifting "set"), which succeeds in an erasing or ignoring of external *and* internal reality. Isolation and repression by themselves accomplish an effective distancing of responsibility; isolation means setting something apart, at least apart from feelings and conviction; repression means pushing something from within the mind (never completely separable from the external something to which it is attached) out of consciousness altogether. (Actually, all defense mechanisms—an arbitrary classification of the defensive functioning of the mind—accomplish some disowning; the relevant question for each individual is: how much?)

Defensive mechanisms culminating in a disowning of responsibility can be conscious or unconscious, operating with some exercise of will or automatically. These defensive sets can be transient operations—we are always censoring psychic input from without and from within the body and mind—or relatively fixed, as the result of confirmed prejudices, characterologically determined (neurotic) good or bad expectations, or "delusions"; we all have a dynamic range of mixed varieties. They can operate in the service of maintaining primal narcissistic delusion—attempt to affirm omnipotence, immortality, and permanent benevolent care from godlike parents.

Patient E was trying to work out some distancing from his mother and father. His adult functioning was, for the most part, excellent. He was a very eligible bachelor, a handsome man always accompanied by beautiful and interesting women. He appeared to be highly successful in a series of business ventures which required considerable ingenuity. Some of these had involved occasional sharp practices and borderline dishonesty, but E felt that his partners were responsible for these ethically questionable areas which were barely acknowledged. He never asked himself or his partners questions about them and felt little or no responsibility for them; he did not want to know. On the few occasions when the businesses were threatened by lawsuits, he had felt transient panic, but this was quickly succeeded by his predominant sense of confidence and self-righteousness. Somehow the crisis would be resolved, and it usually was—sometimes by him, more often by others. E was left unscathed but unable to learn from experiences that he had barely registered; and so he was unprepared for the next time.

It follows that he occasionally ignored or denied problems that needed solutions—solutions he usually would have been well able to work out himself but often left to others, who lacked his talents. This had led to some unfortunate setbacks, to the dismissal of partners, and even to the loss or change of business ventures over the years. What looked superficially like burgeoning success—the undertakings had become more and more ambitious and lucrative—on closer examination seemed always to have involved unnecessary risks and juggling on the edge of collapse. Several times collapse had been avoided only through the ready, eager interventions of financial rescue by E's wealthy parents.

In spite of his superior abilities when functioning as a responsible adult, E at times felt the panic, helplessness, and worthlessness of a dependent child. On these infrequent occasions, he ignored his problems and could scarcely use his intellectual gifts; sometimes he had found it necessary to call on one of his partners to take over for a while. E acted like a child more often than he allowed himself to know. He was surprised by his regressions and reactions when he could not ward off experiencing the fear and powerlessness of a child, and he quickly "forgot" it all afterward. Because his narcissistic vulnerability was not usually apparent to others, E easily reassured himself that what he had felt and what had happened didn't "count."

The distressing feelings were recurrent, as were masochistically provocative actions aimed at creating crises which seemed unconsciously designed to effect parental intervention. Essentially, E denied these recurrent sequences. There was a partial and very inadequate recording in memory of his feelings and actions. Either they hadn't occurred (delusion) or they had no meaning (quasi-delusion) or they would never occur again (near delusional, predominantly unconscious dishonesty). Characteristically, insofar as his "official" recognized conscious persona reigned, E felt righteous and superior, the master of his fate. But beneath this hovered dim feelings of fraudulence, malfunction, and expectations of disaster in spite of what his friends kept reassuring him was remarkable success. This distant but simmering awareness, together with some fear of his conscious goals of marriage and fathering children (what he wanted to want) and mortification about a particularly painful failure of one of his businesses had led him to try psychoanalysis.

It turned out that he not only characteristically distanced and disowned events that threatened him in his professional life but also handled similarly any failure, moral lapse, or deficiency of character (anything that involved narcissistic injury) in his social and sexual life. Essentially it seemed to me that E led the superficially generally successful life of a narcissistic, overindulged (spoiled and naughty), masochistically provocative child—without much responsible awareness of this. He could not say no to himself as an adult, just as his parents had been unable to say no to him as a child. He would declare, smiling, with an attempt at charm, "I'm just a child," but this was aimed at an audience and not *owned*.

E was acutely sensitive to narcissistic manifestations and lack of responsibility in others, but he seemed unable to see himself in these others. He hated those in whom he unconsciously saw himself; but he was also attracted to people who were narcissistic and manipulative. They were supposed to change and become loving and giving toward him and then to rescue him, as his parents had promised always (and frequently had managed) to do. He was almost invariably disappointed when the self-serving nonparental others predictably did not put him first and fulfill his wishes. The propensity for this kind of "transference" contact had led to his making bad judgments, which precipitated some of the intermittent failures he had an unconscious stake in creating, and it was part of the obfuscated but discernible psychology of a loser lurking behind the formidable facade of E's success. Only his superior intelligence and considerable seductive charm directed toward the right people (sometimes carefully, sometimes luckily, selected) had enabled him somehow to appear to be and even to become a winner. But there was also a continuing and intense unconscious stake in losing—failure would deliver him over to his rescuing parents to form the symbiotic union promising immortality and bliss that had endured from his early childhood. Mother and father, and the parental figures onto whom they were temporarily transferred, were the only people who consistently seemed to matter for him. The dependency on his parents (quickly shifted onto his analyst) seemed intermittent because it was so intense that he had to minimize or deny it. Before he started his analysis, partners, friends, and lovers were at best fleetingly meaningful. E enacted with them—but it was mainly a kind of theater: it made him appear to be adult and normal. It looked *as if* he had an exciting and engaged life. But beneath the facade lurked vague and transient feelings of heartsickness, emptiness, despair, and incipient panic.

E's regressive actions and feelings (of narcissistic promise and of infantile dependency) were reinforced by constant telephone contact with his wealthy and overconcerned parents (themselves overindulged, grown-up children), whom E had endowed—following their coercive praise and promises and their inability to refuse their only child anything—with the magical power to get him out of any trouble. He paid for this by the unconscious masochistic need to get into trouble so as to maintain the narcissistic promise. It seemed clear to me that E clung to his narcissistic delusions so tenaciously because this was his way of denying the eventual separation from and loss of his parents. (I think this observation can be generalized to understand a basic need for everyone to cling to narcissistic delusions.)

Any manifestation of parental weakness or illness, any slight refusal or rejection on their part both terrified and infuriated E. Over the course of some years in analysis, he had begun to grasp something of the nature and cost of his dependency. He then spontaneously decided to decrease the frequency of phone calls and visits to his parents (they lived in another country), but the craving for contact continued, and sometimes—especially after some achievement that meant being separate, sexual, adult, responsible— there was an impulse to undo: to visit them or at least to call to tell them his troubles or ask for a gift—an impulse that he could not or would not control. This was a repetitive sequence that the analyst had repeatedly pointed out. (The defensive purpose of the enaction was usually easy for the patient to grasp, at least intellectually afterward.) In the periods before contacting them, E usually appeared to have once again lost all responsibility for the effects such contacts had on him. After renewal from the narcissistic and delusional parental, primarily maternal, source ("*We* are the great people" was one of his mother's mottos), E would in effect become his mother—or at least one of his internalized versions of her—full of infantile, narcissistic, polymorphic perverse but essentially sadomasochistic fantasies, impulses, and sometimes even actions. But there was no conscious responsible knowledge of the identification with her.

Late in the analysis, after some modifying changes had occurred, E started an analytic session depressed and weeping. "I feel that I have lost my mother, really lost her," he declared. This was said in a tone of voice that I learned often denoted a delusional or quasi-delusional mode of mental operations. I felt that his tears were real but that E was also expressing himself histrionically, in an exaggerated, unconvincing moan; he seemed to be at some emotional distance not perhaps so much from his sadness, as from a conviction of having truly lost his mother. This session followed one in which he reported having had a very enjoyable sexual experience during which his partner had seemed precious and lovable to him. This unusual, intoxicating, but frightening feeling had even lasted for a considerable time after his orgasm. But then the good feeling had been succeeded by gloom and, the next morning, by a turn toward functioning masochistically and provocatively both toward his girlfriend and in his business—a characteristic "negative therapeutic reaction" against maturational progress that threatened change and therefore loss of the dependent masochistic and narcissistic delusional ties to his parents. He had then become aware that meaningful feeling for his girlfriend meant somehow that he had lost his mother. He felt like a sad, frightened, deserted child. By the time E expressed them to me, these initially devastating feelings of loss seemed to me to have defensively taken on considerable as-if quality.

> ANALYST: What threatens you is not that you have lost your mother but that you have had some realization that one day you will lose her.
> PATIENT: Yes, that is true. It is more that I feel as if I have lost her, but I realize now that what I am trying to deny is death itself. [This sounded sincere, like E's adult, nondelusional mode.]

There followed a long silence. Then the patient became agitated:

> What I just said to you about death was intellectual—I was mainly repeating after you. But it was only *as if* my mother could die—although maybe I had felt it differently before coming into the hour. But then, just now when I was quiet, I began really to

feel it. She really could die. People die and they never come back. She really could, it's not *as if.* And now I can't stand it. [E began to tremble.] I *do* have to deny that death is real.

E was to regress again, repeatedly. But here he seemed to have achieved a temporary containing (in the presence of the analyst) and therefore an owning of his intense fear of losing his mother, of the possibility of her death, and his own. By this time the analysis had, slowly and with many regressions, brought E to the point of being able to know about and to relax his dissociating "delusional" defenses sufficiently to feel and (hardest of all) to begin to consolidate and register his dangerous, hostile, fearful emotions.

Alongside an increasing ability to separate from his parents and to acknowledge the possibility of irreversible loss, E had become increasingly able to enlarge upon and eventually become responsible for his previously only glancingly mentioned perverse fantasy life and the attenuated enactment of these fantasies. He showed less tendency to generalize his sexual sadism and to project it onto me ("Everybody does and feels things like this, and you do too!"). Since puberty, he had been wont to feel that his polymorphically perverse, largely sadomasochistic arousals and his experimenting with perverse contacts in actions that were never fully consummated didn't count—the events would never happen again, he would never masturbate to such sick fantasies again, and so on. Resolution after resolution failed, but the break with reality was sufficient for him not to, as Freud says, "get securely hold of" this in any effective way: the next time simply would be different. He would arrive at the "conviction" that he was really sexually sound and now had really grown up and put "that stuff" away for good. Delusion repeatedly triumphed.

After years of the analyst's gently, but firmly, mirroring the patient's obsessive repetitions with descriptive interpretations of his sophisticated and subtle defensive range of denial involved in disowning, E finally began to be responsibly aware of and, intermittently, to correct the deficient registration of his patterned compulsive, frequently perverse, sexual ways. He started one day to speak in a different way about his occasional sadistic practices with casual pickups:

> PATIENT: As soon as I've had an orgasm, what I have done and felt no longer exists. I usually get away from the woman as soon as I can. It is as if I blow it all away in one instant. It's that way with masturbation with the fantasies too. And yet, the next time, I feel I really have to do it. I can't give it up. I have no feeling of being responsible or that I can control it. And yet I don't take that seriously.
>
> ANALYST: Aren't you implying that you don't know if you can control it or not?
>
> PATIENT: I feel that I really can control it, but I really don't know. I keep saying to myself, "It's not my fault; it's not my fault." My God, I sound like the Vicomte de Valmont.

E didn't explain his reference. I knew that the well-educated patient was referring to one of the main characters in the great eighteenth-century psychological novel *Les Liaisons dangereuses* (Dangerous acquaintances), by Pierre Choderlos de Laclos. E had no way of knowing that this was a favorite book of mine; perhaps he assumed I had read it or had seen one of the movies made from the novel.[1] What he was referring to comes from a letter that the cynical Vicomte de Valmont writes to the virtuous married woman Madame de Tourville, whom he had seduced with his astute, psy-

---

1. It would have been characteristic (*and delusional*) for E to assume, at least intermittently, that I as the omnipotent other who was (or was almost) his other self of course knew everything he knew. A fantasy of merged omnipotence was slowly and responsibly acknowledged (owned) late in the analysis.

chologically calculated lies. He had tricked her into going to bed with him by convincing her of his love for her. In spite of his characteristic resolve to the contrary, her essential goodness and genuine love had moved him to value her and even to love her. Valmont was jeered at for this "weakness" by his fellow conniver (and ultimate betrayer), the sadistically cruel and power-hungry Marquise de Merteuil. The threat of the marquise's disdain injured his narcissistic vanity. She was not only a former lover but had functioned as a parental alter ego; her disapproval brought the danger of the loss of a narcissistic tie to a maternal figure by whom he felt challenged but whom he felt he needed. (Together they were "we superior beings," as E's mother used to say.) The narcissistic and symbiotic need triumphed, and Valmont repudiated his adult love for the good and caring Madame de Tourville. He sent her a copy of the following text, dictated to him in a letter by the similarly narcissistically threatened and malignantly envious[2] Marquise de Merteuil. She knew him well enough to be sure he would follow her covert suggestion to make use of it to end his affair. (At the behest of the mother-figure he broke with his beloved and returned to the symbiotic attachment nourished by his narcissism.) Here is the letter:

2. Envy is the enemy of love, and malignant envy in its murderous intensity wants to murder love. "Love shall not triumph," melodiously cries Medea in her tragic ambivalence in Cherubini's opera. The psychological danger of object loss, of narcissistic object loss, is too much for her. To lose her husband, Jason, to his new bride means she will lose everything. Medea must be the only child and will murder all rivals. (She had already killed her brother in order to save Jason and help him escape from her father.) Medea, capable of cruelly murdering her innocent rival without a qualm ("O shriek of grief! Voice sweet to my heart!"), is in torment because she feels she must kill her sons ("Figlie miei, miei tesor"), her "treasure," dismissing them in her envious rage and craving for revenge as *his* children. Stabbing them and showing Jason the bloody knife ("They were your children!"), she succeeds in murdering her love as well as her sons.

One gets bored with everything, my angel; it is a law of nature. It is not my fault. If therefore I am bored today with an adventure which has occupied me entirely for four mortal months, it is not my fault. If, for example, my love was as much as your virtue— and that is certainly saying a lot—it is not surprising that the one was over at the same time as the other. It is not my fault. It follows from this that for some time I have been deceiving you; but your pitiless fondness forced me to in some way. It is not my fault. Today a woman that I love madly insists that I sacrifice you for her. It is not my fault. I realize that this is a good opportunity to accuse me of perjury: but if nature has only given men assurance while she has given women obstinacy, it is not my fault. Believe me, choose another lover, as I have taken another mistress. This advice is good, very good; if you find it bad, it is not my fault. Goodbye, my angel. I took you with pleasure; I leave you without regret. Perhaps I shall come back to you. So the world goes. It is not my fault. (1782, 404–05; my translation)

The letter breaks Madame de Tourville's heart; she sickens and dies. And then Valmont, after discovering that he has been betrayed by the marquise, and motivated also by grief and guilt over losing the love he had tried to disown, provokes a duel in which he allows himself to be killed. He is in a real sense murdered by the envious marquise, who could not bear his love toward a rival. Love challenges the narcissistic philosophy she has steeled herself to be movivated by, and it breaks the symbiotic bond to Valmont, her mirrored masculine self. And also, like Medea, she cannot forgive the narcissistic humiliation of being abandoned.

I think this letter is an eloquent example of not owning feelings—of separating out and rejecting some of the emotions (here Valmont's love) involved in threatening conflict. Loving and hating are isolated, thoughts and emotions are dissociated (E. M. Forster would say the prose is disconnected from the passion), and what triumphs (transiently but tragically for Valmont, who has really been changed by his experience of love and who subsequently cannot forgive himself for what he has done) is regression to what Forster calls the "undeveloped heart."[3]

Some time after this session I pointed out to E, at a time that seemed appropriate, what I felt was his protective tendency to use general designations rather than provide details about the sadistic fantasies and actions he reported (usually in a kind of confessional). Didn't this provide for him a kind of emotionally isolated state, a container, as it were, disconnected from his other thoughts and feelings and therefore from the communication of those linkages in the analysis? "Yes," he answered without hesitation, "I real-

3. Margaret, in *Howards End* (Forster 1910), is aiming to change her future husband's undeveloped heart: "It did not seem so difficult. . . . She would only point out the salvation that was latent in his own soul, and in the soul of every man. *Only connect!* That was the whole of her sermon. *Only connect the prose and the passion,* and both will be exalted, and human love will be seen at its highest. *Live in fragments no longer.* Only connect, and the beast and the monk, robbed of the isolation that is life to either, will die" (174–75, my italics). Forster uses the phrase "undeveloped heart" in an essay on the English character that is applicable to the very French Vicomte de Valmont (whose actions are not those of the typical man, let alone the typical Englishman) since it has to do with the more universal, although individually as well as nationally varying, cultivation of emotional isolation as part of what I have called elsewhere (Shengold 1989) "anal-narcissistic defense." An extreme and typically English version may have been commonly found in the English public school boys about whom Forster writes: "They go forth into a world of whose richness and subtlety they have no conception. They go forth into it with well-developed bodies, fairly developed minds, and undeveloped hearts. And it is this undeveloped heart that is largely responsible for the difficulties of Englishmen abroad. An undeveloped heart—not a cold one. . . . For it is not that the Englishman can't feel. He has been taught at his public school that feeling is bad form. He must not express great joy or sorrow, or even open his mouth too wide when he talks—his pipe might fall out if he did. He must bottle up his emotions, or let them out only on a very special occasion" (1920, 5).

ized somewhere that telling the details might make it all count. And then I would have to give it up. And then I would get panicky. If I give it up I will have nothing. That's crazy; it's as if I'm afraid of my whole sexual life being taken away from me." (What E had to connect to was not only the expectation of castration but the perverse, largely sadomasochistic impulses in relation to his mother— impulses so full of murderous feeling that they meant the unbearable loss of her, including loss of her as part of himself.)

What seemed to allow for the beginning of owning these interpretations of his functioning was the changing nature of E's transference onto me as analyst. He began to register and acknowledge the focusing of his sadomasochistic expectations and distrust and hatred after he had attained some ability to care about me and to trust that I would not respond to his seductions and would not be killed off by his hostile feelings and wishes. The approach toward holding onto me with love was accompanied by E's growing ability to tolerate and be more consistently responsible for (own) his distrust toward me. This ability to hold in his mind the contradictory feelings that he repetitively and compulsively felt toward me began to interweave with a similar ability to be responsible for his contradictory feelings toward his mother, with whom he had confounded the analyst (= a "transference"). The empowering "transference love" (Freud has pointed out that all love is basically transference love) paradoxically also had a delusional component (as it generally does). But, over time (as in ordinary human development), the love became less idealized and intense and more realistically founded. The delusions of my perfection and omnipotence faded, as did those of my monstrous destructive power; his real or imagined defects became tolerable and registerable and could be owned, as could his deficiencies and impulses. And a more consistent genuine (but of course still intermittent) caring for me as a separate human being became discernible.

The repetitive defense interpretations aimed at helping E to see the subtle, effective, and self-destructive means he used to achieve his disavowals and denials (and specifically to see their delusional intensity and effect) began to take hold only when E was somehow roused (at first transiently and with quick regressions) to an active curiosity about himself. "I am becoming a real analytic patient," he accurately observed; he also appeared to be on his way to becoming a real "mensch." This increasingly effective intellectual activity, which engaged his emotions and provided motivation, marked a weakening of the hitherto powerful ban on taking his perceptions, thoughts, and feelings seriously. He could see, he could know, he could begin to own awareness of the defects of his analyst, his parents, the God who up to now he felt was looking after him. Most important of all, he was starting to own the defects in himself. This meant a great attenuation, but of course not the disappearance, of the narcissistic delusions which never can be completely given up. But part of my functioning as analyst—I feel a most important part—was my being able to grasp and therefore to help E see how widespread and powerful, how inhibitory and even destructive, and, above all, how "delusional," how destructive of ordinary reality his defensive disowning was. Grasping this was only one step, but perhaps it was the decisive step in E's hard struggle in analysis to own and to attenuate the power of the dissociated fantasies, memories, and feelings and wishes that had distressed and frightened him so. He also needed to renounce or at least weaken the masochistic and perverse activities that furnished gratifications (the motivational carrot, as it were, in addition to the stick of intense anxieties) and kept him in servitude to the omnipotent rescuing parents he felt he couldn't live without (and had to preserve by narcissistic delusion). He had to give up the promise of his and their immortality and omnipotence. His most difficult hurdle was becoming able to feel and acknowledge the terrifying murderous intensity of his hostility. So, gradually, separation and maturation were made possible, and identity was furthered. Love was permitted as hatred became more tolerable; the good and the bad both could be registered and integrated as good-and-bad[4]— and there was less fear in feeling "That's what I feel; that's who I am."

This case has featured transference delusions—the coming into focus of the past (in the specific form of the narcissistic delusions that fuel the delusions of everyday life) on the person of the analyst and the work of the analysis. Freud likens the transformations of aspects of the buried past that occur in the course of analytic transference to the infusion of blood into the ghosts in the *Odyssey*—bringing them to life and therefore subject to one's responsible awareness. (To paraphrase the epigraph from Freud to this chapter: you must bring your ghost to life before you can acknowledge and exorcise it.)

Transference phenomena are full of delusion, for everyone. (It is to be remembered that transferences are ubiquitous—present in every situation in life as well as in treatment.) These are often quasi-delusions: "I know you really won't marry me, but I expect you will all the same," one young woman patient said to me. But full-blown, even psychotic transference delusions—transient or more fixed—are not uncommon. Of course some are there before the treatment starts; the ghosts spring instantly to life with the beginning of contact with the analyst, or even its anticipation.

After the publication of my book on adults who had been subject to abuse in childhood, *Soul Murder,* I received many requests for consultation from readers who felt that their feelings and expe-

4. "For Rickie suffered from the Primal Curse, which is not—as the Authorized Version suggests—the knowledge of good and evil, but the knowledge of good-and-evil" (Forster 1907, 197).

riences were reflected in the book. At that period, I had no free time in my practice for new patients and explained this before I consented to see those who wanted consultations. One man responded that this was just what he wanted; he did not have the money for treatment and simply wanted to get my advice—my book was so fine, he said, that he was sure it would be good advice. However, once he was in my office, it was clear that he expected, despite what I had said, that I would see him in therapy. I quickly grasped that it was not advice he was seeking but a magical source of miraculous change. He wanted also to vent his complaints against God and all his nearest and dearest, especially his parents. Indeed, he had a terrible story to tell, of mistreatment and rejection from childhood to the present—but I had no way of knowing how much of it was true because the way he presented himself, as misunderstood and mistreated by everyone he mentioned, persuaded me that he must be paranoid. Every tentative and gentle attempt at advice on my part was indignantly brushed aside as unempathic and ridiculous. At the end of the hour I told him that I felt I had been of little help to him. He clearly grasped that he was being dismissed and that I was not going to continue to see him. He became intensely animated and engaged in what seemed to be a triumphant diatribe:

> I knew this would happen. I knew you were one of those doctors who write about people so nicely but really don't want to help them at all. You make millions from your books and take advantage of all your suffering patients. I knew that someone who writes about dead authors so much isn't really interested in live people. Shengold, I will ruin your reputation!

He left the office with a blissful smile. For him the paranoid delusion quickly sprang to life, seemingly without any possibility of his owning it.

For less disturbed patients, like E, much working with defenses is still necessary to accomplish the first (and what sometimes is the crucial) step of helping the patient to make the delusion manifest. That is just the beginning of mutual work to convert the (usually) transient appearance of delusion into material the patient can become responsible for and own as part of the self that has resulted from, and is maintained by, conflicts from within the mind. (It is usually the achievement of owning that takes most time in the therapy.)

Hans Loewald has something characteristically wise to say about delusions in the "normal":

> A psychotic core, related to the earliest vicissitudes of the ambivalent search for primary narcissistic unity and individuation, also is an active constituent of normal psychic life. . . . These deeper unconscious currents, having been uncovered and reentering modern sensibility, influence the organization of mind, experience and action. . . . Our psychotic core, as it comes increasingly into view, prevents us from being as much at home and at ease with . . . our normal form of organizing reality, aiming at a strict distinction and separation between an internal, subjective, and an external, objective world, as our scientific forefathers were. (1978, 403)

(This description of the ubiquitous normal difficulty with differentiating objective reality implies a normal tendency toward delusions and quasi-delusions.) Loewald continues,

> Just as the Oedipus complex, the neurotic core, wanes but is never actually or definitively destroyed, and rises again at different periods in life and in different shapes, so, too, that more archaic, psychotic core tends to wane but remains with us. Indeed the Oedipus complex and its sequelae, viewed prospectively rather than retrospectively from adult life, are later versions of archaic,

yet enduring, indestructible life issues. In normality the psychotic core is harder to find than the Oedipus complex; in the classical neuroses it may not need specific analytic work. . . . In the psychosexual and social life of the present day "archaic" currents are more in evidence, less repressed, I believe. They consequently make for different troubles, often closer to "perversion" than to neurosis. (400, 403)

I would add, and therefore closer to delusion (see chapter 6).

In the following passage from an earlier paper (1977), Loewald is referring, I believe, to narcissistic transference delusions:

One can speak, following Kohut, of narcissistic transference—or self-object transference—insofar as there is a relatedness, a rapport between patient and analyst, *which is mainly based on an archaic form of relatedness, close to or reproducing "symbiosis,"* and which is repeated in or transferred to the analytic situation. There is transfer of the archaic relatedness, with its blurring or lack of ego boundaries, from the pre-oedipal prototypes to given current figures and specifically to the analyst. By virtue of the undifferentiated nature of this transference such patients have difficulty not only in distinguishing between themselves and the analyst but also between infantile and current figures, between infantile or archaic and current, more advanced levels of relatedness: not only the differentiation of internal and external, but also that of past and present is deficient. (217)

In a previous chapter, I reminded the reader of the potential delusional nature of resistance as well as of transference. (What Loewald calls the "psychotic core" furnishes the most difficult resistances to changes in life and in psychoanalysis.) Freud describes and classifies resistances in psychoanalytic treatment which represent in a discernible form inner resistances to the free flow of thought and feeling toward discharge in consciousness. Freud's first assumption was that such resistances stemmed from that controlling and executive part of the mind he called the ego, which has to mediate between the need to obtain satisfaction of impulses on the one hand and the need to avoid dangers on the other. Later he added resistances stemming from the id and the superego. In 1926, Freud wrote,

> It is hard for the ego to direct its attention to perceptions and ideas which it has up till now made a rule of avoiding, or *to acknowledge as belonging to itself* impulses that are the complete opposite of those which it knows as its own. Our fight against resistance in analysis is based upon this view of the facts. If the resistance is itself unconscious, as so often happens owing to its connection with the repressed material, we[5] make it conscious. If it is conscious, or when it has become conscious, we bring forward logical arguments against it; we promise the ego rewards and advantages if it will give up its resistance. (159; my italics)

For the ego—the "I"—"to acknowledge [unpleasant and threatening impulses, perceptions, ideas, and emotions] as belonging to itself" is a good way to define *owning*. The acknowledgment can be painful and hateful, but it means knowing as much of what is there and what was there as can be borne; and that is a giant step toward attaining identity, authenticity, and the ability to love.

---

5. Most analysts today would say that this "we" *should* mean the analyst and the patient. (It is not completely clear that Freud means that here; he appears to be using the royal "we," which would indicate the work of the analyst alone; certainly this is the way he uses "we" as the paragraph proceeds.) It is the patient's active exploration, guided by the analyst's interpretations of resistance and of what is being defended against but is on the edge of the patient's conscious perception, that is effective in first acknowledging and then working through toward what Freud describes as the ego becoming able to own the previously repressed or consciously disavowed material.

I have in this chapter and repeatedly in previous ones stressed that in order to change we have to own what we are and what we are stuck with. The narcissistically based need for certainty and its opposite—the impossibility of being certain about anything—are probably there to some extent in all of us; they are two sides of the same coin, and infinite individual varieties of the two are possible. The intensity of need for this certainty usually arises for purposes of defense—to avoid or deny changes that bring about too much stimulation, too much pain. When held to with compulsive force, the need for "delusional" certainty or uncertainty makes it impossible or at least extremely difficult to accept changes—past, present, and future. One cannot without strong motivation and great struggle own what lies outside and threatens these areas of compulsive certainty. Therefore they are central to the human tendency to resist change.

My main purpose in writing about the remnants of primal psychic functioning in everyday life is to express the conviction that what I have loosely called delusions and quasi-delusions furnish much of the power for the more persistent and effective resistances to change in life and in psychoanalysis. The "delusions," as I have repeatedly stated, are attempts to preserve narcissistic attributes of fixity and changelessness: no passage of time, no death; no separations, no losses—having everything and being parented forever. I have given clinical illustrations in passing and will add a few short examples here. These are not instances of chronic delusions or of chronic functioning that would warrant a diagnosis of psychosis. The "delusions" are transient, but they recur persistently, in characteristic patterns. Their appearance and use are usually enhanced, often to the pitch of phosphorescence, by the regressive concentration of emotion that occurs so regularly in psychoanalysis or psychoanalytic psychotherapy—a regression that mobilizes primitive defenses as well as primitive intensities. The return to aspects of the earliest mental functioning is resorted to when one is threatened with the developmentally determined psychic danger situations listed by Freud (1926), especially by the earliest ones: traumatic overstimulation and separation from mother (primal parent); these are the basis for the others. I have oversimplified these dangers by lumping them together as "life without mother." (I have found it effective to do this in communications to patients.)

There are an infinite variety of intrapsychic conflicts which lead to danger situations that evoke regressive "delusionary" reactions in order to cling to the past and resist change and loss. Each person however has an individual pattern that the analyst and the patient need to get to know. One patient would predictably reestablish a narcissistic state by announcing something like, "It's all over. You aren't even here in the room with me anymore. You don't exist!" This patient was used to saying such things and could take it lightly. She did not know at the start that the words were accompanied by a shift in consciousness, a kind of autohypnosis, that, indeed, meant a definite emotional withdrawal—a disowning—that effectively reduced the universe by psychically eliminating the analyst, who stood for the world outside her mother's orbit. Autohypnosis, which can be subtle enough to make its use sometimes unknown to the patient and hard to detect by the analyst, is often used to achieve narcissistic delusion and to disown what might threaten its sway. Similar reversion to past psychic states can be achieved by psychic merger (also "delusional" and accomplishable by shifts in consciousness). One patient was wont to state, "I feel as if you have become part of me," or, more subtle, "You already know what I am going to say." (The latter also brings in the related delusion of the analyst's omniscience and projection of the patient's own delusional omniscience.)

Characteristic projections make for the paranoia of everyday life. Another patient would say, "I know *you* think I am being dishonest here," when warding off responsible consciousness of his own prevarication and deceit. A characteristically tardy patient would repeat, "I know you hate me for my lateness." It was a long time before she could appreciate that this was not just a casual repetitive statement ("Oh, I didn't really mean it!") but a delusional conviction that had successfully, despite lip service to the contrary, warded off her actually feeling her intense hatred for me as the one who had the power to keep *her* waiting. It was harder for her to grasp and therefore to own the delusional element in the, again, repetitive statements such as, "I know it's crazy but I feel that you are a monster." Only through the analyst's dealing equally repetitively with trying to uncover the specific wardings off that this kind of announcement attempted to accomplish (and also the shift in consciousness announced by the changed and "sleepy" tone in which such disclaimers were pronounced) was it possible for the patient to grasp how effective such projections were and get to the threateningly deep feelings they were designed to block. Such recurrent feelings, full of primal intensities, can also be avoided in many other ways that can involve "delusion," for example, by actions that discharge them—or through silences (if there is autohypnosis here, as there frequently is, the analyst cannot sense it directly). These resistances, since they are bolstered by "delusions," are difficult to analyze because they are difficult to own. Awareness of the inevitable presence of these "everyday delusions"—learning to expect them—makes the analyst's or therapist's work easier. But the patient must be or become willing to give them up.

It follows that the analyst must also be conscious, in the task of monitoring his or her own emotional tendencies toward the patient and reactions to the patient's associations (potential or activated countertransferences and counteridentifications), of the warning signals and hallmarks of the analyst's own "delusions" and quasi-delusions. Because these are based on shared human narcissistic predilections, they are frequently infectious—like the patient's yawns. They can be called counterdelusions, and awareness of their onset can sometimes serve as a valuable signal that can lead, with some self-analysis, to what is going on in the mind of the patient.

Because we are tied to the power of the conditions and conflicts that adhere to what I have loosely called narcissistic delusions, we are tied to the past in ways that compromise our future. This is true because the human compulsion to repeat experiences of traumatic intensity and the easy defensive resource to regression in the face of painful affects make for revivals of the past. Freud has rightly described neurosis as a projection of the past onto the present and future. This has a constricting effect. Our present and future are depleted by the fixed universe and needed certainties of the distant past. Primitive mental functioning is marked by oversimplification and certainty in the course of what Sandler (1987) has called a search for safety. The safety is needed, in my view, in large part as a consequence of instinctual drives that force us toward overstimulation in the form of potentially unbearable affect. To be able to bear the early intensities we require a certain amount of psychic structure and functioning at birth (and the absence of defects in that structure and functioning), but above all we need the help of a mothering person over years of intense psychic dependence. That this maternal care will and must continue forever, that life without it is impossible, is the nidus for narcissistic delusion. We cannot help seeking in our concepts of death and the mystery of what lies beyond it the narcissistic certainty of the moments of timeless safety and perhaps also of bliss from our earliest existence. We can never quite give up the quest for this experience of "everything and forever" and its defensive counterpart—a fixed and eternal order.[6]

6. In *Halo in the Sky* (Shengold 1988), I have written of the universal need for order in the form of obsessive-compulsive structure based on what I have called anal narcissism.

But these needs must be distanced in order to achieve a meaningful existence as an adult—an existence that requires flexibility and not fixity, an emotional openness and moderation rather than all-or-nothing emotional intensities that brook no compromise, a facing of the unknown (good-and-bad) rather than what has already been. To embrace change and master the external and internal worlds, to the extent that these can be mastered, we must distance the terrible emotional intensities, the heaven and hell, of primal psychic life. And accommodation to change is necessary as well as desirable—it gives us a present and a future: somewhere to go in addition to where we have been. Inexorable fate demands it, and we have only delusional denial to turn to, a turn we all make to some extent and mainly intermittently—but such psychotic denial of the conditions of life inhibits whatever mastery of those conditions we can achieve. And, paradoxically, it is the internal necessity as part of human nature for holding onto some quanta of our primal psychic inheritance that supplies an intensity needed for power, "drive," and zest. This dangerous, potentially destructive intensity must be maintained within optimal bounds (perfervid narcissism reduced to "intimations of immortality")—an accomplishment dependent on the achievement of the ability to care about ourselves and others. It is emotional flow of these primal intensities that provides not only the miseries but also the joys inherent to being human.

CODA

The primal psychic world—the infant's and child's preoedipal world—is full of delusion and hallucination. For most people, hallucinations fade as childhood recedes; they are not significantly present for most adults except pathologically in the psychoses and certain organic conditions and states (for example, toxic states) affecting the brain; and physiologically: universally present in dreams, there for some in the transitions between sleeping and being awake, and in states of extreme stress or emotional intensity.[7] Freud writes (in *The Interpretation of Dreams*) about hallucinations of the psychotic and of the normal:

> It should be remembered . . . that it is not only in dreams that such transformations of ideas into sensory images occur: they are also found in hallucinations and visions, which may appear as independent entities, so to say, in health or as symptoms in the psychoneuroses. (1900, 535)

At this time Freud included the psychoses as part of "the psychoneuroses." Hallucinations in the "normal" are comparatively rare. But delusions—most characteristically evident in the quasi-delusional form I have described (for example, "I will never die")—are common. They frequently exist as unconscious assumptions. The unconscious mind, where timelessness reigns and there is no death —partly inherited and partly established by the internalization of the external preoedipal world—also develops related "delusional" conscious and preconscious manifestations. The persistent and regressive psychotic-like phenomena are disguised by later transformations as well as by other defensive psychic developments in the course of maturation.

In the primal infantile psychic world, feelings have an all-or-nothing quality, one of the characteristics of primal affects that are linked to the "delusional" mode. These exigent feelings are (or can become, if development proceeds badly) too much to bear and must be tamed and neutralized by the acquisition and transformation of various defenses that begin to flower as the mind develops and matures. But often, in the earliest narcissistic period of mental

7. For example, believing one sees on the street someone close to one who has just died.

development, or later (especially if there is traumatic enhancement of the inevitable too-muchness, or if some inherent organic deficiency is present, or as a result of bad parenting and bad internalization of parental care), the defensive system that is necessarily primarily directed against body feeling and emotions either does not develop sufficiently or becomes hypertrophied with a consequent squeezing out of emotion. For those whose psychic emotional sphincter remains too much associated with repressive anal sphincter control (see Shengold 1988), psychiatric treatment aims at making the release of repressed and suppressed emotions tolerable. We would want such patients first to feel, then to be able to retain awareness of their emotions and body feelings. For those who tend to feel too much, we need to help nourish or encourage the attainment or maturation of psychic structure that can dampen down and reduce both the fluidity and the intensity of affect. Both kinds of patients (the underdefended and the overdefended) need to learn to tolerate a whole range of contradictory feelings, bad as well as good feelings and the interaction between the two;[8] optimally they should become able both to be playful with feelings and to take them seriously. They are to become emotionally free insofar as this is compatible with retaining enough control; this means that the freedom and fluidity of emotions have to be limited and anchored by the individual's gradually and predominantly becoming able to take responsibility for them. There can be too much freedom and playfulness. Both infantile overfluidity and overdefensive rigidity can restrain growth and maturity, inhibiting the acquisition of wisdom, perspective, and tolerance of the inherent limitations of life (of the ordinary misery Freud referred to as

8. Patients frequently have great difficulty in simultaneously feeling anger and love—it can be frightening or even terrifying (depending on the intensities) to hate the person you love and need.

our unanalyzable human burden imposed by our nature and our fate). We must achieve a separate identity—see who we are, and with whom we are and where we are going—in the service of a separation—a condition in which there may occasionally, and of course will eventually, be no others. And this must become at least transiently bearable; otherwise we will call on narcissistic delusions and can become mired in them.

Think of the mysterious, dynamic, often fragile,[9] contradictory complexities that make for the establishment and maintenance of a sense of identity. There are so many components. One must first establish boundaries of the body—between the self and the external environment. Identity is formed first from shifting and relatively fixed identifications with others, beginning with the parents: conscious, unconscious, partial, primal or primitive, mature (acquired by transference), and so forth. As we mature, coalescences of functions and splits (splits as pictured in our theoretical models of the structure of the mind) develop, giving rise to our hypothetical psychic structural entities: the unconscious (part of which is the repressed), the preconscious, the conscious; id, ego (conscious and unconscious), superego (conscious and unconscious). These are horizontal splits in our "psychic apparatus" models in which the separate parts of the mind can be envisioned in interplay (cooperation and conflict) in both normal and pathological mental functioning. There are also mental splits that are nearer to what can be found clinically—that is, these are at least in part potentially experiential and can rise to conscious awareness. I will classify them loosely:

1. Those that are splits in the mind (if pictured, these splits would be vertical); these are flexible—that is to say, dynamic

9. In states of relative psychic health dynamic structures are both flexible and resilient and their fragility fades.

and transformable or reversible—and are part of ordinary conflictual as well as relatively conflict-free mental functioning: self as subject and self as object; observing self and experiencing self; splits in the conscience: "yes" parts and "no" parts providing praise and punishment, respectively.

2. Those that are fixed and pathological vertical splits of the mind or parts of the mind:

a. The contents of the repressed (part of the unconscious ego).

b. Aspects of the self that can appear in consciousness but are dissociated, isolated, and sometimes projected onto others; vertical splits in self and object mental representations, which can range from transient phenomena to multiple personalities.

I will not add to this inadequate and arbitrary list. Defining and tracing the vicissitudes of the sense of identity is an impossible goal, and it would need a separate book of encyclopaedic detail and size even to attempt it. What is a sense of self, of I, of me? Questions are perhaps more meaningful than answers here. And poetic brevity can probably do better than the scientist's more encompassing attempts:

Do I contradict myself?
Very well then I contradict myself,
(I am large, I contain multitudes). (Whitman 1851, 102)

In this same poem, *Song of Myself,* the self-examining narcissistic poet has the marvelous line, "I am the man, I suffer'd, I was there" (1851, 76), which can be seen as emblematic of owning one's past.[10] Of course it is easier to declare the owning in words and in a work of art than to achieve it in life.

10. Whitman is also very much aware of the difficulties and complexities involved in achieving a sense of identity:

In psychoanalytic theory and treatment we focus on two pervasive mental mechanisms, introjection and projection (taking in
and casting out), as a kind of basic medium to try to understand
the development of a person's separate self and mind and the
worlds external to it (first the world of the body, and then the
world external to the body). The mind's registration of other people and the interplay with them are of primary importance in
maturation—alongside some inborn maturational scheme.

We become ourselves partly by way of mysterious inborn organic maturational givens that interconnect with the environmental
forces—the external world (general conditions needed for human
survival and especially those influences imposed by and gradually
acquired from our primary caretakers). We identify with our parents, first in some sort of primal, relatively undifferentiated fashion
and then in more complex and differentiating ways. It is this need
to preserve the original universe—environment and self—that constitutes the primal tie to the parents. The need for parenting is
probably inborn and probably has the quality and certainly the
force of an instinctual drive (see Jacobson 1993).[11] *It is above all*

When I read the book, the biography famous,
And is this then (said I) what the author calls a man's life?
And so will some one when I am dead and gone write my life?
(As if any man really knew aught of my life.)
Why even I myself I often think know little or nothing of my real life,
Only a few hints, a few diffuse faint clews and indirections
I seek for my own use to trace out here. (1867, 1875)

11. If viewed either as an inherited instinctual drive or not, the inevitable
exigent need for parenting would of course interplay with the sexual and aggressive
drives from the beginning of mental development—there is no separate or separable (except for heuristic purposes) line of development or any either/or possibility here. Sex and aggression make for the attachment to the parent. I am sure
that Jacobson would agree with this.

this need to hold onto the primal parent as the link to life and to death as immortality that makes for the narcissistic delusions—fragments of which are visible in adults as the delusions of everyday life. One can view Freud's hypothesis of biologically based life and death instincts in terms of the need to separate from (life) and re-merge with (death) the primal parent. If we can own the tragic distance from the promise held out by these delusional intimations of immortality, we can achieve the restorative human powers that can mark the acceptance of the fall from paradise—and can consider, with Milton's fallen angels,

. . . our own loss how repair,
How overcome this dire calamity,
What reinforcement we may gain from Hope,
If not what resolution from despare. (I:188–91)

APPENDIX 1

A NOTE ON

SYMBOLISM

· · · · · · ·

The use of symbolism and language makes our minds flexible enough to grasp, master, and communicate thoughts and feelings. What we master is in large part the primal mental functioning that leaves its remnants in the delusions of everyday life.

Symbolism is an enormous, complicated, and significant topic; I am not attempting any definitive summary or literature review and am merely offering a point of view. I recently published a book containing a chapter on the symbolic meaning of the shoulder (Shengold 1991). The shoulder as a linguistic symbol referring to the actual body part can, like any element from the world external to the mind, be used as a metaphor for anything, although of course not always happily. (Lionel Trilling says that Freud teaches us that the mind is a poetry-making organ, but it doesn't always make good poetry.)

Vann Spruiell, with whom I discussed my ideas on the symbol of the shoulder, said to me with his usual mixture of honest impatience and cogency, "I'm sick of these papers that say a symbol means this or means that; anything can stand for anything." He is of course right. But his statement applies to linguistic (ordinary verbal) symbols, which come relatively late in the mind's (and symbolism's) development. Spruiell was specifically referring to the clinically verifiable fact that any symbol can stand for any important aspect of mental development—can have, for example, an oral, anal, phallic, and genital (male and female) meaning, as well as referring to aspects of ego and object relations development (although, again, not always with "poetic" felicity).

Freudian (unconscious) symbolism is a more controversial subject. Does it make sense, in the light of current evolutionary theory, to think of symbols as having some phylogenetic derivation? A more practical question: is it clinically useful to give the shoulder (in addition to its myriad metaphoric possibilities as a linguistic symbol) one or a few relatively fixed and unvarying meanings that would be universally employed by the unconscious mind—which would make it a Freudian symbol? My answer to the latter question is a qualified yes, and I have tried to defend it at length and specifically in relation to the shoulder (on the basis of material from myths and clinical material) in my book (1991).

In the primal period of equating symbolically what is inside and outside the mind, during which unconscious Freudian symbols are established, an erogenic part of the body comes to be represented by a part of the object world. During the process of body ego formation, after boundaries have been established, objects from the external world are taken into the mind (and "recorded") by being equated symbolically with those within the body. The initial universe for the infant that we picture as chaotic (as in *Genesis*) becomes in subsequent development the universe of the child's body blended with the body of the primal parent. Gradually the mental grasp and picture of the universe expands (after body ego formation and separation from the breast/mother) to include two parents and siblings; then the universe centers around the nursery. (By a developing process of Metaphor we take in our approximation of the outside world!) As the mind develops and transforms its initial primitive method of functioning (primary process to secondary process) the world gets larger and larger and the ego (now psychic ego with body ego "alongside and beneath") shrinks, although (paradoxically and poignantly) the mind now can contain (insofar as the mind can contain) registrations of the "real" universe.

If, with the symbolic equation that makes for Freudian symbolism, a pencil is unconsciously equated with the phallus, the pencil can be treated (because of its unconscious evocation of erogenic and aggressive feelings) as if it *were* a phallus. The pencil, operating as an unconscious symbol, would have acquired an exigency that would be manifested in excitations, avoidances, symptoms, perversions, and so forth.

At some early time (after the primal chaotic period of psychic development) when some psychic structure, contents (mental representations), and boundaries have been established, the body itself exists as one of the two worlds external to the mind (the other being the world external to the body). At that point psychic representations of certain parts of the body can be used defensively as places on which to displace clamorous, drive-invested representations of erogenic body parts like the mouth/breast (later the differentiated mouth [me] and breast [not-me]), anus, and genitals, which are so subject to psychic conflict. I call this equating of the more indifferent body part to one that is instinctually charged "displacement symbolism."[1] For example, the knee can (and Freud says does) function as a symbol for the genitals, the leg can symbolize the penis. I view these displacement symbols, regarded developmentally in time, as intermediate between the (late) linguistic or word symbols and the more primal Freudian or unconscious symbols—as defined by Freud and others (see Fliess 1973).

1. I was chagrined to find in the course of writing this coda that Robert Fliess, in his book *Symbol, Dream and Psychosis* (1973, 41–43), has employed this term (which he attributes to Freud) in much the same way I have. I had evidently forgotten having read it there, and in my (1991) book claim it as my own.

Freud contrasted "dream symbols" (unconscious symbols which he differentiated from other—easily made conscious—ordinary word or mathematical or musical symbols) as being both phylogenetically derived and not acquired through learning:

> It seems to me, for instance, that symbolic connections, which the individual has never acquired by learning, may justly claim to be regarded as a phylogenetic heritage. (Freud 1916–17, 199)

Freud also claims that patients do not associate to these symbols in dreams. This is obviously not literally true. It would be better stated that patients do not necessarily in their associations arrive at *the* unconscious meaning of the symbol in the manifest content of the dream (unless they have already read or been told of its unconscious "analytic" significance).

The shoulder, like the cigar, can also be just a shoulder; but when it is used as a linguistic symbol it can have many meanings. In contrast, I am asserting that the shoulder, as an unconscious symbol (when defined either as a Freudian or as a displacement symbol), represents cannibalism: the devouring mouth and/or the devoured breast. This primal (and universal) meaning can and does accompany and qualify later (anal, phallic, genital, other) meanings. In a previous book (1991) I have tried to document this with myths from Greek literature (compare the myths involving Tantalus and Pelops) and from the Bible and with clinical material (for example, shoulder biting in love play). I was also reminded, when I presented a paper based on my material at the Western New England Psychoanalytic Society, that the currently popular and undoubtedly cannibalistic myth of the vampire (see Gottlieb 1991) usually involves biting the part of the neck that is proximal to the shoulder.

Some of the discussants added their own clinical observations in which the shoulder was associated with oral sadism; also, several remarks were made that suggest some backing from ontogenetic development for the idea that shoulder comes to stand for cannibalism and the subject and object of cannibalism. Dr. Stephen Atkins observed that the breast is for feeding while the shoulder is for burping, for the interruption of feeding. Being held against the shoulder is usually comforting but does not necessarily remain so for the really hungry or colicky infant—whereby it can acquire the meaning of frustration.[2] The shoulder is rounded like the breast but lacks the soothing and exciting (another paradox) oral contact provided by the nipple and cannot furnish (although initially it might promise) the satisfaction that can ultimately come only from milk. The shoulder can therefore conceivably be experienced, and sometimes repeatedly experienced, by the infant as a frustrating, anger-inducing breast. Rosemary Balsam reinforced this by telling of a hungry baby in the second year of life and in the process of being weaned who regularly bit her mother's shoulder.

In the course of analytic associations, the analyst will frequently encounter the shoulder as an object to be bitten: "When I get up off the couch to leave the session, I'd like to pounce on you sitting in the chair there and bite into your shoulder," said a female patient who had been expressing great dissatisfaction about her femininity. She would frequently rouse her husband from sleep to intercourse by biting him from behind on the shoulder. She mentioned watching lions mating on a television program and was excited by the lion's holding the lioness in place by seizing her shoulder in his teeth. This is apparently a regular sexual practice of the large cats. (In this multidetermined example, there are, as is usually the case, obvious references to more than the oral developmental level.)[3]

2. Anyone who has held a hungry infant on his or her shoulder (it is easy to forget—this is a grandparentally derived note) will have had the experience of the baby rooting at the shoulder for a nipple—sometimes urgently.

3. For example, this analyst's first name is derived from *lion*.

If the symbolic equation between the shoulder and cannibalism that I have suggested is accepted, one could try to account for it phylogenetically. Our animal nature predisposes us to bite, and the shoulder is among the tastiest parts of the animals carnivores eat. But the ontogenetic explanation provided by the discussants at New Haven seemed to me convincing enough to publish this addition to what I have already said on the subject.

Giving a positive answer to the question of the clinical usefulness of Freudian (unconscious) symbols per se—that is, Freud's ideas (1900, 1916–17) of dream symbolism and symbolism as a primary process mechanism—seems to me to be dependent on *whether,* and especially *how,* the primitive mind functions differently in relation to symbolism than does the developed mind (see Lear 1990). (The importance of the different modes of functioning is the underlying assumption of this book.) I can state with a fair degree of certainty that the archaic mind does work differently, but the *how* is more controversial. And many analysts have tried to sketch out the way this is reflected in symbolism (for example, Kubie 1953).

I agree with Robert Fliess, who justifies the use of Freudian unconscious symbols as follows:

> There are . . . instances in which an analyst finds that for him a symbol translation, not communicated to the patient, illuminates a previously meaningless series of associations. (1973, 19)

(But of course it must be added that to be certain that the illumination is valid and not primarily a projection of the analyst, the patient must at some point supply the material [optimally, beforehand] that can lead to and/or verify the analyst's intuitive grasp, arrived at or enhanced by the unconscious symbolism involved.) I hope that my symbolic equation of the shoulder will prove to be useful along these lines. I feel convinced myself both of the specific unconscious symbolic meaning of the shoulder and of the clinical usefulness for understanding that can be supplied by unconscious (Freudian) symbolism.

APPENDIX 2

. . . .

"People Like You and Me": Relevant Quotations from Randall Jarrell's *Pictures from An Institution*

Randall Jarrell's wise, humane, and wonderfully funny novel *Pictures from An Institution* presents a northeastern American women's college (a kind of Sarah Lawrence or Bennington he calls Benton) as a picture of mid-twentieth-century "progressive" academia. It is a specific, idiosyncratic microcosm, but one that reflects and epitomizes a much larger world. The novel illustrates a social milieu that clearly, wittily, movingly demonstrates the delusions of everyday life—present not only in the academic eccentrics but as part of being human—in you and me, as Jarrell says. I hope these few quotations will motivate the unacquainted reader to seek out this marvelous, inexhaustibly playful, perpetually readable book.

The narrator is trying to show someone new to Benton the exotic peculiarities, individually different in detail yet shared in kind, that mark the majority of the faculty there, that supply an aura. He alludes humorously to his reactions to the Benton atmosphere in a playfully exaggerated depiction of a typical faculty member:

> Sometimes you meet, coming down the leafy path along which you are walking, a man dressed as Napoleon; as he talks to you you look at him with distrust, pity, and amusement—carefully

do not look, rather. But as the two of you walk along, and people come up with wallpaper designs full of imperial bees, rashly offer their condolences on the death of the duc d'Enghien, ask for a son's appointment as Assistant Quartermaster-General of the army being sent to the Peninsula, you realize that it is not he but his whole society that has "lost touch with reality." (87)

Here the narrator, himself a poet (like Jarrell) and a professor at Benton, is addressing a temporarily visiting professor, the novelist Gertrude Johnson, who is trying to pump him for "facts" she can use in the satirical novel she intends to write based on the people at this college, new to her. The narrator describes Gertrude to the reader as a writer with a "Freudian" bent whose novels aim to expose everyone's bad motives:

She knew without half trying the secret of every alcove, and could hardly look at a baby without saying to the mother something about polymorphous perversity [64]. . . . She said to the Universe that she accepted it, for Analysis [188]. . . . She was a mousy woman till she smiled—torn animals were removed at sunset from that smile. [65]

Gertrude (she is said to be based on Mary McCarthy; this is Jarrell's own roman à clef about academia) both fascinates and repels the narrator. In discussing one odd faculty member, Dr. Willen, formerly at Morford College, now in Benton's Psychology Department, the narrator is simultaneously telling Gertrude the truth, keeping her amused, and poking fun at her:

"[Dr. Willen] lost her job at Morford for cooking a hen on a Bunsen burner."

(Gertrude:) "For *what?*"

"She was doing experiments in visual perception, stuff with color wheels, and spending most of her afternoons and evenings at school. She got tired of having to go home so much, so she just slept on the cot in her office, half the time, and cooked dinners in her lab. But she was domestic, and the dinners got pretty elaborate. One night she was so proud of a hen she'd roasted, with dressing and everything, in a sort of Dutch oven arrangement over some Bunsen burners, that she went along the hall and knocked at all the office doors that were lighted and got two graduate students and a professor to come have dinner with her. They talked quite a lot about it. Of course, that hen was just the straw that broke the camel's back; she'd done plenty of queerer things. . . . But it was bound to happen with *some* psychologist; psychologists love teas. And physiologists—biologists in general. Though mostly they're sort of graham cracker and banana teas."

(Gertrude:) "Are they all so—eccentric?"

"Psychologists? Pretty often—some of them are odd to begin with, and that gets them interested in psychology. But the rest are the—the—soberest of men."

(Gertrude:) "I didn't mean the psychologists, I meant professors in general."

"Most professors aren't a *bit* eccentric. They're just like—'*just like you and me*,' I had started to say, but somehow this seemed the wrong thing—"businessmen who've gone into teaching and got unbusinesslike. Or tame Roman emperors—they *are* sheltered, in their late days. I know one old one that—you'd know him, he edited *The White Devil*—that put up the window and called to some boys that were making too much noise: 'Begone!' One of them right here—Dr. Savitt, the one that's the expert on Lincoln—has made a lot of money in real estate, and is a bank director, and I knew one who was paid by the National Association of Manufacturers to go around making speeches to Chambers of Commerce, and never washed; and the man I took geology with lectured in iambics, and used to talk about Geological

Determinism. And I knew one who raised mocking birds from their shells, without their mothers, so as to prove their songs were inborn—and to prove the inheritance of acquired characteristics he raised two dachshund puppies that sat up and begged before their mother taught them, but they died. People are much more eccentric than they're supposed to be. But dully so. Of course some professors are—" then I paused, feeling that I should have done so hours before, and said more sensibly, "It's like people. People aren't like anything, there are too many of them. Professors aren't like anything, they're like everything. I'm a professor; why, Gertrude, right now, you're a professor." (96–98)

Later on the narrator expands on this train of thought to the reader:

Most of the people of Benton would have swallowed a porcupine, if you had dyed its quills and called it Modern Art; they longed for men to be discovered on the moon, so that they could show that *they* weren't prejudiced toward moon men; and they were so liberal and selfless, politically, but what words of men, or tongue of man or angel can I find adequate to this great theme? In the world outside one met many people who were negatives of the people of Benton: exact duplications, but with the whites and blacks reversed. There were people who thought anything but calendars and official portraits Modern Art, and spoke of it with exasperated hatred; people who wrote to the Chicago *Tribune* to denounce it for the radical stand it had taken on some issue; people who said resignedly, when their big summer houses, on cliffs overlooking the sea, had fewer closets than they liked: "But that's not the arcitect's fault—*that* comes from being poor." They moved you to moralize almost: as you looked at them you realized better the quixotic charm of the people of

Benton, whom you could laugh at with an untroubled—a less troubled heart. You felt about the people of Benton: *If only they weren't so complacent! If only they weren't so*—then you stopped yourself, unwilling to waste an afternoon on *if only's*, and mumbled a summary *If only we were all dead or better!* Though this was unjust to the great mass of people, normal in-between people with nothing much wrong with them, people like you and me; well, not us exactly, but us if we were different. (104)

We are, alas, not different.

REFERENCES

· · · · · · ·

Abraham, K. (1920). Manifestations of the female castration complex. In *Selected Papers of Karl Abraham*, 338–69. London: Hogarth Press, 1949.

——. (1921). Contributions to the theory of the anal character. In *Selected Papers of Karl Abraham*, 370–92. London: Hogarth Press, 1949.

Blum, H. (1980). Paranoia and beating fantasies. *J. Amer. Psychoanal. Assn.* 28:331–63.

Boyd, B. (1990). *Vladimir Nabokov: The Russian Years.* Princeton: Princeton Univ. Press.

Butler, S. (1841–86). *The Family Letters of Samuel Butler,* edited by A. Silver. Stanford: Stanford Univ. Press, 1962.

——. (1871–85). *Letters between Samuel Butler and Miss E. M. A. Savage, 1871–1885,* edited by G. Keynes and B. Hill. London: Jonathan Cape, 1935.

——. (1874–83). *The Notebooks of Samuel Butler.* Volume 1, edited by H-P. Breuer. New York: Univ. Press of America, 1984.

——. (1874–1902a). *The Notebooks of Samuel Butler,* edited by H. F. Jones. London: Hogarth Press, 1985.

——. (1874–1902b). *Samuel Butler's Notebooks,* edited by G. Keynes and B. Hill. New York: E. P. Dutton, 1951.

——. (1899). *Shakespeare's Sonnets Reconsidered and in Part Rearranged.* London: Jonathan Cape, 1927.

——. (1903). *The Way of All Flesh.* New York: Macmillan, 1925.

Calef, V., and E. Weinshel. (1981). Some clinical consequences of introjection: On gaslighting. *Psychoanal. Q.* 50:44–66.

Chekhov, A. (1904). *The Three Sisters,* translated by R. W. Corrigan. In L. Trilling, ed., *The Experience of Literature,* 205–40. New York: Doubleday, 1967.

Cooper, A. (1986). What men fear: The facade of castration anxiety. In *The Psychology of Men,* 89–106. New York: Basic Books.

Cooper, A. (1993). Paranoia: A part of most analyses. *J. Amer. Psychoanal. Assn.* 41:423–42.

Crabbe, G. (1816). *Crabbe's English Synonymes.* New York: Harper and Bros., 1917.

Dickens, C. (1853). *Bleak House.* New York: Doubleday, 1953.

Eckermann, J. (1836). *Conversations of Goethe with Eckermann,* translated by J. K. Moorhead. London: Everyman's Library, J. M. Dent, 1930.

Fliess, R. (1953). The hypnotic evasion: A clinical observation. *Psychoanal. Q.* 22:225–30.

———. (1954). The autopsic encumbrance. *Inter. J. Psychoanal.* 35:8–13.

———. (1956). *Erogeneity and Libido,* International Universities Press.

———. (1973). *Symbol, Dream and Psychosis.* New York: International Universities Press.

Forster, E. M. (1907). *A Room with a View.* New York: New Directions, 1922.

———. (1910). *Howards End.* New York: Vintage, 1985.

———. (1920). Notes on the English character. In *Abinger Harvest,* 3–14. New York: Harcourt, Brace, 1936.

Frank, A. (1969). The unrememberable and the unforgettable: Passive primal repression. *Psychoanal. Study Child* 24:48–77.

Freud, S. (1887–1904). *The Complete Letters of Sigmund Freud to Wilhelm Fliess. 1887–1904,* translated and edited by J. Masson. Cambridge: Harvard Univ. Press, 1985.

———. (1900). The interpretation of dreams. *S.E.* 4, 5.

———. (1905). Three essays on the theory of sexuality. *S.E.* 7.

———. (1909a). Analysis of a phobia in a five-year-old boy. *S.E.* 10.

———. (1909b). Notes upon a case of obsessional neurosis. *S.E.* 10.

———. (1910). Leonardo da Vinci and a memory of his childhood. *S.E.* 11.

———. (1913). Totem and taboo. *S.E.* 13.

———. (1914). On Narcissism. *S.E.* 14.

———. (1916–17). Introductory lectures on psychoanalysis. *S.E.* 15, 16.

———. (1917). A childhood recollection from *Dichtung und Wahrheit. S.E.* 17.

———. (1921). Group psychology and the analysis of the ego. *S.E.* 18.

———. (1923). The ego and the id. *S.E.* 19.

———. (1925). An autobiographical study. *S.E.* 20.

———. (1927). The future of an illusion. *S.E.* 21.

———. (1930). Civilization and its discontents. *S.E.* 21.

———. (1933). New introductory lectures on psycho-analysis. *S.E.* 22.

———. (1937). Analysis terminable and interminable. *S.E.* 23.

——. (1938). Findings, ideas, problems. *S.E.* 23.

——. (1940). An outline of psycho-analysis. *S.E.* 23.

——. (1960). *Letters of Sigmund Freud,* edited by E. Freud. New York: Basic Books.

Gottlieb, R. (1991). Clinical Data and Legend. The European Vampire. Paper presented at a meeting of the Psychoanalytic Association of New York, February 25, 1991.

Graves, R. (1955). *The Greek Myths.* Baltimore: Penguin Books.

Green, A. (1969). *Un Oeil en trop: Le complex d'Oedipe dans la tragédie.* Paris: Aux Editions de Minuit.

Greenacre, P. (1963). *The Quest for the Father: The Study of the Darwin-Butler Controversy as a Contribution to the Understanding of the Creative Individual.* New York: International Universities Press.

Grossman, L. (1993). The perverse attitude toward reality. *Psychoanal. Q.* 62:422–36.

Grossman, W. (1993). Pain, aggression, fantasy and concepts of sadomasochism. *Psychoanal. Q.* 62:22–52.

Grünberger, B. (1971). *Narcissism: Psychoanalytic Essays.* New York: International Universities Press, 1979.

Henderson, P. (1954). *Samuel Butler: The Incarnate Bachelor.* Bloomington: Indiana Univ. Press.

Henseler, H. (1991). Narcissism as a form of relationship. In *Freud on Narcissism: An Introduction.* New Haven: Yale Univ. Press, 1991.

Jacobson, J. (1993). Developmental aberration, multiple modes of the mind, and the therapeutic relationship in psychoanalysis. *Psychoanal. Q.* 62:523–52.

Jarrell, R. (1954). *Pictures from an Institution.* New York: Alfred A. Knopf.

Jones, H. F. (1919). *Samuel Butler: A Memoir.* 2 vols. London: Macmillan.

Klein, M. (1946). *Envy and Gratitude.* New York: Basic Books, 1957.

Kouretas, D. (1963). L'homosexualité du père d'Oedipus et ses conséquences. Athens: Privately printed reprint from *Annales Medicales.* Sept–Dec, 1963.

Kubie, L. (1953). The distortion of the symbolic process in neurosis and psychosis. *J. Amer. Psychoanal. Assn.* 1:55–86.

Laclos, C. de. (1782). *Les Liasons dangereuses* (Dangerous acquaintances). Paris: Gallimard, 1972.

Lear, V. (1990). *Love and Its Place in Nature: A Philosophic Integration of Freudian Psychoanalysis.* New York: Farrar, Straus, & Giroux.

Lewin, B. (1946). Countertransference in the technique of medical process. *Psychosomatic Medicine* 13:3–10, 1940.

———. (1948). The nature of reality, the meaning of nothing, with an addendum on concentration. *Psychoanal. Q.* 17:524–26.

Loewald, H. (1977). Instinct theory, object relations, and psychic structure formation. In *Papers on Psychoanalysis,* 207–19. New Haven: Yale Univ. Press, 1980.

———. (1978). The waning of the Oedipus complex. In *Papers on Psychoanalysis,* 384–404. New Haven: Yale Univ. Press, 1980.

Mahler, M., and B. Gosliner. (1955). On symbiotic child psychosis. *Psychoanal. Study Child* 10:195–214.

Meissner, W. (1993). Vincent: The self-portraits. *Psychoanal. Q.* 62:74–105.

Milton, J. (1669). *Paradise Lost.* In *The Student's Milton,* edited by F. A. Patterson, 153–363. New York: F. S. Crofts and Co., 1946.

Mitchell, S. (1993). Aggression and the endangered self. *Psychoanal. Q.* 62: 361–82.

Nabokov, V. (1966). *Speak, Memory: An Autobiography Revisited.* New York: Putnam, 1966.

Novick, J., and K. Novick. (1991). Some comments on sadomasochism and the delusion of omnipotence from a developmental perspective. *J. Amer. Psychoanal. Assn.* 39:307–32.

Orgel, S. (1994). A psychoanalyst's reflection on Chekhov and *Three Sisters. Inter. J. Psychoanal.* 75:133–48.

Orwell, G. (1949). *Nineteen Eighty-Four.* New York: Harcourt Brace.

Ovid (A.D. 10). The story of Narcissus. In *Metamorphoses. Book Three,* translated by J. Addison, 85–87. New York: Heritage Press, 1961.

Pascal, B. (1630–62). *Pensées,* translated by M. Bishop. In Morris Bishop, *Blaise Pascal,* 165–256. New York: Dell.

Peto, A. (1959). Body image and archaic thinking. *Inter. J. Psychoanal.* 440: 223–31.

Raby, P. (1991). *Samuel Butler: A Biography.* Iowa City: Univ. of Iowa Press.

Rilke, R. (1952). *Letters on Cézanne,* translated by J. Agee. New York: Fromm, 1985.

Russell, F. (1925). Introduction to Butler, S. (1903), *The Way of All Flesh,* v–xv. New York: Macmillan, 1925.

Sandler, J. (1987). *From Safety to Superego.* New York: Guilford Press.

Sandler, J., and B. Rosenblatt. (1962). A concept of the representational world. *Psychoanal. Study Child* 17:128–48.

Scott, W. (1805). "Lay of the Last Minstrel." In *The Complete Poems of Walter Scott,* edited by H. Scudder, 47–80. New York: Houghton Mifflin, 1900.

Segal, H. (1973). *Introduction to the Work of Melanie Klein.* 2d ed. New York: Basic Books.

Shakespeare, W. (1597). *Romeo and Juliet.* In *The Oxford Shakespeare,* edited by W. J. Craig, 882–918. New York: Oxford Univ. Press, n.d.

———. (1623). *Macbeth.* In *The Riverside Shakespeare,* 1307–42. Boston: Houghton, Mifflin, 1973.

Shengold, L. (1963). The parent as sphinx. *J. Amer. Psychoanal. Assn.* 11:725–51.

———. (1978). Autohypnotic watchfulness. *Psychoanal. Q.* 47:113–20.

———. (1981). Insight as metaphor. *Psychoanal. Study Child* 36:289–306.

———. (1988). *Halo in the Sky: Observations on Anality and Defense.* New Haven: Yale Univ. Press, 1992.

———. (1989). *Soul Murder.* New Haven: Yale Univ. Press.

———. (1991). *Father, Don't You See I'm Burning?* New Haven: Yale Univ. Press.

———. (1993a). *"The Boy Will Come to Nothing!"* New Haven: Yale Univ. Press.

———. (1993b). Oedipus and locomotion. *Psychoanal. Q.* 63:20–28.

———. (1993c). A note on symbolism. A brief communication. *Inter. J. Psychoanal.* 74:961–64.

———. (1994). Malignant envy. *Psychoanal. Q.* 64.

Sheridan, T. (1747?). Memoir of Dean Swift. In *The Choice Works of Dean Swift,* ix–lxxxii. Boston: DeWolfe, Fiske and Co., n.d.

Sophocles. (Date unknown). *Oedipus Rex,* translated by R. Jebb. In *Seven Famous Greek Plays,* edited by W. Oates and E. O'Neill, Jr., 117–82. New York: Modern Library, 1950.

———. *Oedipus Rex.* In *The Oedipus Cycle,* translated by D. Fitts and R. Fitzgerald, 1–78. New York: Harcourt Brace, 1949.

Spruiell, V. (1975). Three strands of narcissism. *Psychoanal. Q.* 44:577–93.

Swift, J. (1726). *Travels into Several Remote Nations of the World. In Four Parts. By Lemuel Gulliver.* In *The Choice Works of Dean Swift,* 3–178. Boston: DeWolfe, Fiske and Co., n.d.

Tolstoy, L. (1886). The death of Ivan Ilyich. In *Tales of Courage and Conflict,* edited by C. Neider, 368–410. Garden City: Hanover House, 1958.

Trilling, L. (1955). Freud: Within and beyond culture. In *Beyond Culture,* 89–118. New York: Viking Press, 1965.

Webster's New World Dictionary of the American Language. College Edition (1953). New York: World Publishers.

Whitman, W. (1851). *Leaves of Grass.* New York: Modern Library, 1921.

Wordsworth, W. (1807). Ode. Intimations of immortality from recollections of early childhood. In *The Poetical Works of William Wordsworth,* edited by T. Hutchinson, 587–90. London: Oxford Univ. Press, 1923.

INDEX

· · · · · · · ·